PLYMOUTH ARGYLE

A FILE OF FASCINATING FOOTBALL FACTS

MIKE BLACKSTONE

GW00326484

Best wishes

Mike B—

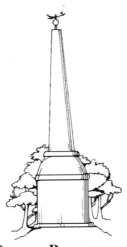

OBELISK PUBLICATIONS

ALSO IN THIS SERIES:
Torquay United – the First 70 Years, Laura Joint
Exeter City–a File of Fascinating Football Facts, Mike Blackstone

ACKNOWLEDGEMENTS

Grateful thanks are given to the many people who have assisted with the preparation of this book, but in particular to the staff of the Exeter Central Reference Library, Plymouth City Library and the gentlemen of the Press who have so faithfully over the years reported and recorded the history of Plymouth Argyle Football Club through the medium of newspapers, radio, and television. A special mention should made of Harley Lawer of the Sunday Independent who has followed the fortunes of the Argyle for many years and researched the Club's history. It has enabled me to check and double check those early club statistics and anecdotes with my own records.

The following newspapers in particular have all proved to be invaluable whilst researching the history of the Club. They are: The Express & Echo, Western Gazette, Western Morning News, Western Evening Herald and, of course, The Sunday Independent. Copies of Programme Monthly Magazine have also been consulted.

I should also like to thank Sam Rendell of Plymouth Argyle for his greatly appreciated assistance and knowledge of the Club. To Dave Fisher, Phil Stoy, Ray Dack, Phil Hiscox and John Hannaford for allowing me access to their notes and recollections of Plymouth Argyle.

Photographs have been obtained from a number of sources including Sunday Independent, Plymouth Argyle Football Club, Chips Barber, Dave Fisher and Tony Ellis. Special thanks to Dan McCauley, Chairman of Plymouth Argyle Football Club, for his support and encouragement.

Finally thanks are also extended to Jim Blackstone, who has collected and collated football statistics and stories with me for a number of years. We have spent countless happy hours together delving into the past history of the world's greatest game, much to the chagrin of the rest of the family!

Statistical information included in the book is up to date as at 1st October 1992.

BOOKS ALSO ABOUT PLYMOUTH AREA FROM OBELISK PUBLICATIONS:
Plymouth in Colour, Chips Barber
The Great Little Plymouth Book, Chips Barber
Walks in Tamar & Tavy Country, Denis McCallum
Walks in the Shadow of Dartmoor, Denis McCallum

For further details about these or any of our other titles about Devon, please contact us at 2 Church Hill, Pinhoe, Exeter EX4 9ER, Tel: 0392 68556

First published in 1993 by
Obelisk Publications
2 Church Hill, Pinhoe, Exeter, Devon
Designed by Chips and Sally Barber
Typeset by Sally Barber
Printed in Great Britain by
Sprint Print Company Ltd.
Okehampton Place, Exeter.
Tel: (0392) 433570

INTRODUCTION

"A Football Club with enormous potential that has never been quite fulfilled." That was how Plymouth Argyle was once described, and a pretty accurate description it is too. Argyle are the premier Devon club in terms of achievements, ground, and support, but have still to taste soccer at the very highest levels. Nevertheless it is a club, like so many others, which has suffered its fair share of troubles as well. The early days of the club's existence was something of a financial struggle, but they survived that and the later trials and tribulations along the way. Argyle have also tasted, along with their faithful supporters, occasional championship successes, and cup semi-final appearances.

It is a unique football club, for no other senior club can boast the name of Argyle, familiar to all throughout the game. Unique as well because they are the only Football League club currently playing in home colours of green. Those distinct shirts have been a feature for many years. Argyle supporters are fiercely and proudly partisan, quick to praise, and quick to feel aggrieved if things are not going to plan on and off the pitch.

The history of Plymouth Argyle Football Club is a long and varied one, with all manner of stories appertaining to the club itself, the directors, players, supporters, the ground, paddle steamers, and even the traditional humble pasty! All these topics are covered in this book which brings together the familiar and the more obscure moments that Plymouth Argyle have endured. Some events are happier than others during the ninety years of football which have brought so much pleasure and despair to all who follow them.

ABANDONED

The first ever Football League match believed to have been abandoned at Home Park took place on Saturday, January 14th 1939. Plymouth Argyle's Second Division visitors were Norwich City. The game started on an already saturated pitch following a long spell of incessant rain, resulting in pools of water covering the surface. Players slid all over the pitch being unable to keep their feet, but Plymouth did, however, manage to score once through John Archer. His fourteenth-minute free kick from the edge of the area hit the back of the net via the underside of the crossbar. With play becoming almost farcical at times, the referee finally decided to call a halt to the proceedings in the second half, and the 6,942 spectators went home for an early tea.

Argyle's Division Two fixture at Bury in March 1949 was brought to an abrupt halt in the 68th minute with the score standing at 1-1. Back at Home Park in December 1956, the game against Newport County was abandoned at half time. A visit to Cardiff City in March 1963 was ended early in the 55th minute with the scoreline again 1-1.

Other abandoned games that Argyle have been involved in include a trip to Leyton Orient in the snows of December 1950. With Argyle leading 3-2, referee Mr Sawyer abandoned the game at half time after the Brisbane Road surface had frozen solid, and had become too dangerous to play on. Just two weeks later Argyle's match at Port Vale also fell victim to the grip of the wintry weather. The game was abandoned after 56 minutes with neither team having scored.

Home Park was again in a near waterlogged state for the Football League Cup fourth round replay against Aston Villa in December 1960. With the rain lashing down during the game, the scoreline at the end of ninety minutes was 0-0, but the referee decided to abandon the game and not go into extra time to decide the winners. There was some discussion afterwards with Argyle claiming that the game should be replayed at Home Park because the original tie did not run its full course to include the extra time period, whilst Villa were equally adamant that it should be back on their ground. The Football League agreed with Plymouth and the match took place at Home Park, where supporters saw an eight goal thriller, but with Villa winning 5-3.

Another match brought to a premature halt in February 1978 at Home Park was the Third Division fixture against Bradford City. Exeter-based referee Ron Crabb halted proceedings in the 61st minute with the icy cold wind and sleet making conditions extremely unpleasant. One of the Linesmen for the game, Tony Ellis, also from Exeter, recalls Mr Crabb saying that even one of his watches had seized up in the cold. Mr Ellis took to the field for the start of the second half wearing gloves in a forlorn attempt to keep his hands warm. Bradford City were none too happy with the decision for they were leading 1-0 at the time thanks to a 25th minute goal from David

Referee Ron Crabb abandons a Third Division fixture against Bradford City at Home Park in February 1978.

McNiven, claiming that the conditions were no different to those at the time of kick-off.

One of the more unusual reasons for abandoning a game came in Argyle's Football League Cup first round first leg tie at Chester City in September 1981 watched by a meagre crowd of just 1,759. With less than a quarter of an hour of the game remaining, and evenly balanced at two goals each, Chester goalkeeper Grenville Millington, in attempting to stop a shot from Argyle striker David Kemp, collided heavily with the goalpost. In a split second the posts collapsed! Valiant attempts to repair the damage were to no avail and the referee had no option but to abandon the match.

More recently, in November 1983, Argyle's Third Division match with Wimbledon was called off after just 27 minutes play. This was a more controversial decision, however, for whilst there was a good deal of surface water on the Home Park pitch, the respective managers stated that they were quite happy about playing on. Argyle club chairman Stuart Dawe was also disappointed with the abandonment, the scoreline being goalless at the time, and announced that when the game was replayed, admission prices would be half price as a goodwill gesture towards both the Plymouth and travelling Wimbledon supporters. The Wimbledon team did not show such generosity when the game was re-arranged the following April, as they went away from Home Park 2-1 winners.

ADMISSION PRICES

Admission charges to first team matches at Home Park have of course risen dramatically since the inaugural season of the club in 1903/04. Then it cost just six old pence to stand in the ground, and if you could really afford one shilling and sixpence, then sheer comfort would come your way with a seat in the wing grandstand.

Home Park Adult Season Tickets for the 1947/48 campaign cost as follows: Grandstand £5 5s 0d, Ground £1 11s 6d, Enclosure £3 3s 0d. If you could not afford to buy a season ticket the match by match prices were Grandstand 5s 0d (or the equivalent of 25p today), Enclosure 2s 6d and Ground 1s 3d.

How times change! In the 1961/62 season it cost the princely sum of 2s 6d (or 12½p), to watch Argyle from the Home Park terraces. Thirty years later in 1991/92, the cheapest adult terrace price for an adult was £5.50.

Long delays were experienced at the turnstiles for the first few games of the 1979/80 season, causing some supporters to even miss the kick off. The problem was that terrace admission prices had risen from £1 to £1.30, and fans were not bringing the exact money causing delays in change giving. To alleviate future queuing problems, a change kiosk was set up in the hope that the correct money could be given to turnstile operators.

ATTENDANCES

Even pre-season practice matches at Home Park drew good crowds at one time! In August 1946 for instance, an Argyle team of Probables against the Possibles won 7-2 in front of over eight thousand spectators.

Following discussions between club officials and the local police, a crowd limit of forty thousand was agreed for the F.A. Cup third round tie at Home Park against Luton Town in January 1948. There was room for thirty thousand on the terraces, seven thousand in the enclosure, and a further three thousand seated. Preference for seating tickets was given to existing stand season ticket holders, but within hours of that announcement it was reported in the local Press that 'ticket speculators' were in action in the city. A season ticket holder was offered £5 for the right to use his ticket to purchase a stand seat for the game! The eventual attendance was 36,195 who saw Argyle bow out of the F.A. Cup losing 4-2.

Plymouth Argyle averaged 23,345 spectators to their Second Division matches during the 1952/53 season. This is Argyle's best post-Second World War average attendance figure. Plymouth finished in fourth spot in the Second Division table. Compare that average with the one for season

1990/91 when the figure was 6,851 for Second Division fare at Home Park.

The Argyle board of directors were far from pleased with the attendance present at Home Park for their F.A. Cup third round replay with First Division Birmingham City in November 1960. Club chairman Ron Blindell said: "Only 14,132 watched the game. My directors were appalled at the low gate. There is always an outcry from the public if we fail to put on match winning soccer which the directors are trying their best to give them. If supporters wish to see Division One soccer at Home Park, we must have gates of twenty five thousand."

When did a reserve fixture draw an attendance of 25,648 to Home Park? It occurred on 20th January 1962 for a Football Combination fixture against Mansfield Town. It must been quite an experience for the younger players of both sides who had never witnessed anything like it! There was of course a very good reason for this unusually high attendance figure however. Tickets were on sale for the first time for Argyle's third round F.A. Cup tie against Tottenham Hotspur seven days later.

The first sub-2,000 Football League attendance that Plymouth Argyle played in front of occurred at Merthyr Town's Pennydarren Park ground in January 1928. Only 1,500 spectators witnessed a 4-1 win by Argyle over the hapless Third Division South side. The Pennydarren Park ground is still used, now being home to Conference League side, Merthyr Tydfil.

The last match of the 1991/92 season drew the best attendance to Home Park for five years. Plymouth Argyle needed to win to avoid relegation to

the Third Division, whilst their opponents also needed an equally important victory to earn a place in the end of season divisional play-off. The excellent attendance of 17,459 surprised everyone, and long queues formed outside the ground before kick-off, which was delayed for fifteen minutes to enable everyone to take their places. There were still long queues, however, even with a delayed start, and it was reported that supporters were still trying to gain entrance to the ground some twenty minutes after the kick-off. Sadly for Argyle, they lost 3-1, and thus suffered relegation to the Third Division, (renamed the Second Division for 1992/93).

BOWLS

The Plymouth Argyle playing squad temporarily changed sports for the afternoon in August 1946. They visited the bowling greens in Central Park to take place in a challenge match against the Peverell Park Bowling Club. Argyle lost 94 to 78, but it prompted Alderman R. Oke, who welcomed the players to the game, to say: "If you play in the same way that you have played bowls this afternoon you will find Plymothians warmhearted in their friendship and support."

CHRISTMAS DAY

The first match ever to be played on a Christmas Day by Plymouth Argyle at first team level took place at Home Park in 1903 against Reading in the Southern League. Argyle lost 1-0.

The first Christmas Day away fixture took place four years later, again a Southern League match, at Queens Park Rangers. Plymouth did slightly better by drawing 0-0.

Another goalless draw was the outcome of the Argyle's first Christmas Day Football League match. This was against rivals Exeter City at Home Park in 1920, before a bumper festive attendance of eighteen thousand.

Christmas 1946 saw the Plymouth Argyle team leave Home Park on December 21st and not return until Boxing Day morning! They travelled up to the Midlands to fulfil the fixture at Birmingham City and didn't have the happiest of festive starts, crashing to a 6-1 defeat. After staying overnight in Birmingham, the squad moved on to Manchester the next day, which was to be their base until the Christmas Day game at Manchester City. The Argyle players trained on City's Maine Road pitch. There were plenty of goals again, this time Plymouth losing 4-3.

The return fixture with Manchester City was to take place on Boxing Day which meant that both the Argyle and City party of officials and players had to catch the 5.30 p.m. train to London immediately after the Christmas Day game. They then made their way across London to Paddington to catch the overnight train down to Plymouth, arriving in the early hours of Boxing Day morning. Not the ideal pre-match preparation. Argyle lost once more and again the goals flowed, five of them, with Manchester City claiming three.

Not a happy Christmas for Plymouth Argyle!

Traditional Christmas Day fare at Home Park came to an end in 1954, when Swansea Town shared four goals with Plymouth before an attendance of 14,416. Neil Langham and George Dews scored for Argyle. The very last first team Christmas Day fixture came three years later when Argyle had to journey to Somerton Park, home of Newport County, and were rewarded for their troubles with a 2-0 win before an attendance of 10,680, with George Baker and Jimmy Gauld getting the goals.

Happy Christmas Plymouth Argyle! The best Argyle Christmas Day result in a Football League fixture occurred in 1923, a victory that was even more satisfying than usual, for it was against arch Devon rivals Exeter City. Plymouth rattled in four goals at Home Park without reply with Percy Cherrett (2), Cyril Eastwood and Jack Leslie hitting the target.

Two Plymouth Argyle players have the unusual distinction of making their Football League debuts for the club on Christmas Day. Welshman Walter Price lined up at left back in a 1-1 draw at Home Park against Exeter City in 1924, and inside forward Henry Brown made his bow, again at Home Park, in a goalless encounter against Swansea Town twelve years later.

CLUBCALL

Like most Football League clubs, Plymouth Argyle have their own Clubcall telephone number, which offers daily news, interviews, match reports etc. The club receive a percentage of the revenue generated by the service for every call made to it. This popular service was introduced at Home Park in September 1988, the number being 0898 12 16 88.

CROWD DEMONSTRATIONS

Prolific goalscorer Sammy Black was the subject of a crowd demonstration in the 1920s. The Scots forward was an idol with the Home Park faithful, having joined Argyle in 1924 from Kirkintilloch Rob Roy. His goalscoring ability was second to none, but when stories emanated from the Plymouth Argyle boardroom that the directors were considering selling Black, this incensed the supporters so much that a series of public meetings were held, and a 'Sammy Must Not Go' campaign started. The board backed down, the player stayed, and stayed, and stayed! For he finally left Plymouth in 1938 for Queens Park Rangers after amassing 491 appearances and scoring an impressive 185 goals. It proved that directors are not always right!

CROWD DISTURBANCES

Plymouth Argyle full back Moses Russell annoyed the Luton Town crowd with his style of robust tackling in the Southern League match played at Kenilworth Road in April 1920. One Luton fan was so annoyed that he hurled a stone at Russell, only to miss, but hitting Argyle goalkeeper Fred Craig instead. The unfortunate Craig sustained a nasty cut head, but carried

Moses Russell is the bald-headed gentleman in the back row, third from left. Sammy Black is in the front row, second from right.

on after treatment. Argyle went on to win the game 2-1, and the Luton Town club were later, not surprisingly, censured by the Football League for the stone throwing incident.

Police had to move on a group of Plymouth Argyle supporters from the main grandstand entrance after the Division Three South match at Home Park against Gillingham in January 1927. The game had ended goalless, but as the Gills goalkeeper Ferguson left the field, he protested that he had been struck on the leg by a missile. Ferguson had enjoyed a magnificent match with a series of fine saves to deny Plymouth. The Argyle supporters,

The tough-tackling Moses Russell leads the Argyle team out on to the pitch at Home Park.

frustrated by his solo performance, rushed on to the field at the end of the game and surrounded the player and the match referee, both gentlemen having to be escorted to safety by the police.

In December 1960 Plymouth Argyle were fined £20 by the Football Association and ordered to post warning notices around the ground and in the match programme to the effect that any further incidents could lead to the closure of Home Park. Referee Mr F. J. Bricknell of Exminster, near

Exeter, had reported the club to the Football Association after being spat in the eye by a spectator at the end of the Football Combination game against Bristol Rovers. The Football Association told Argyle that they had reached their decision after taking into account three previous reported cases of misconduct at the ground.

The Home Park ground was sensationally ordered to be closed by the Football League following incidents during the Plymouth Argyle and Huddersfield Town match in February 1961. Argyle won the Second Division game 2-1, but it was the events off the field that dominated the newspaper headlines. A section of the crowd had become incensed with some of the refereeing decisions of Dennis Howell, who was also a Labour Member of Parliament. They threw orange peels, paper cups, and even a bottle on to the pitch and the Police had to quell their high passions. Mr Howell said that someone had spat in his face. The inevitable of course happened, Plymouth were reported to the Football League, the outcome being that Home Park was to remain closed for fourteen days.

With Home Park temporarily out of bounds, Argyle turned to their neighbours Torquay United for assistance. They played their 'home' fixture against Ipswich Town at the Plainmoor ground on Saturday, 18th March. This was to be no happy sojourn for Argyle, however, as the men from East

Several of the players in this photograph of the Plymouth Argyle Football Club of 1973/74 have played for other Devon league clubs. Back row (L to R) Hugh Reed, Chris King, Bob Saxton, Keith Allen, Dave Provan, Peta Balac, Jim Hinch, Milija Aleksic, Neil Hague, Paul Mariner, Alan Rogers, Peter Darke, Colin Sullivan. Third row (L to R) Bill Pearce, Bill Shearer, Derek Rickard, Peter Middleton, Dave Pook, Alan Welsh, Jim Furnell, Mike Dowling, Ernie Machin, Steve Davey, John Hore, Tony Ford (Coach), Graham Little (Secretary). Second row (L to R) Messrs Crookes, B.S. Williams, Deans, Daniel (Chairman), Waiters (Manager), Skinnard, Ford, S. J. Williams, Stuttard (Chief Scout). Front row (L to R) Pat Allen, Robert Cross, George Foster, Mark Nicklas, Stuart Masey, Brian Johnson.

Anglia, who later became Second Division Champions, won 2-1.

Plymouth Argyle fans invaded the pitch during the Boxing Day fixture at Home Park against Queens Park Rangers in 1967. They were disputing a penalty awarded against Argyle, which was duly tucked away for the only goal of the game. The club directors immediately stated that any of the pitch invaders who could be identified would be banned from future matches at the ground.

There were ugly scenes at Home Park during and after the final match of the season in May 1983. Visiting Portsmouth won 1-0, and in doing so celebrated winning the Third Division Championship. Their supporters, however, were nothing short of a disgrace. There were several disturbances on the terraces, which had to be dealt with by the police, and after the game they swarmed on to the pitch where fighting broke out. Damage in and around the ground ran into many hundreds of pounds.

DEVON SET

Only a handful of Plymouth Argyle players have the distinction of appearing for all three of Devon's Football League clubs during their careers. Those who have achieved this rare set, namely playing for Argyle, Exeter City and Torquay United, include Fred Binney, Peter Darke, Jack Davis, George Foster, Dave Hancock, Reg Jenkins, Darren Rowbotham, John Sims, Dave Walter, Peter Whiston and John Wingate.

DIRECTORS

Mr A. C. Ballard, President of Plymouth Argyle in 1932, had many visionary ideas although not always connected with football. He suggested air travel to fulfil away fixtures. He put forward his idea to the Football League pointing out that Plymouth Argyle faced long tedious rail journeys, and that air travel would save not only time, but also players would be better prepared for the games. The Football League Management Committee discussed the idea but in their wisdom did not consider it to be worthy of any further consideration!

However, just to prove his point about air travel, on 15th October 1932, when Argyle were due to play at Stoke City, a party of directors and club officials took to the air, leaving Plymouth on the morning of the match, and returning by aeroplane the following day. The journey, paid for by Mr Ballard, took around two and a quarter hours (in an aeroplane which at one time held the London to Cape Record), while the players had to travel by the usual mode of transport, the train. This took eight hours each way! For the record Plymouth lost 2-0, but no doubt the players had a longer unhappy home journey than Mr Ballard and his colleagues!

The board of directors who guided Plymouth Argyle back into competitive football after the Second World War in 1945 consisted of: Sir Clifford Tozer (Chairman) and directors J. Andrew, E. Dobell, R. Heath, Lt. Col. R. V.

This photograph shows the Plymouth Argyle Board of Directors for 1948. Back row (L to R) Group Captain G. L. Pendlebury, J. A. Chapman, D. James, E. Dobell, A. E. Cload, R. Heath, D. Coles. Front row (L to R) F. G. Leatherby, C. E. B. M. Smith, Sir J. Clifford Tozer, Lt. Col. R. V. Hunt, T. R. Nicholls.

Hunt, D. James, F. Leatherby, A. Manico, T. Nicholls, Group-Capt C. Pendlebury, C. Smith, P. Smerdon and C. Spooner.

Directors of football clubs often come under fire from supporters when results on the field are not all they should be. In September 1968 the Plymouth Argyle board of directors took the trouble of writing in the match programme in an effort to put their side of things. It read – "Directors are not in football because there is any financial advantage. At the present time the directors of this club have made interest-free loans of over £40,000." – It was pointed out that the loans were in addition to the money invested in Plymouth Argyle by the directors in the form of club shares, guarantees on the bank overdraft, and mortgages on players' houses.

In the 1977/78 season, following a string of poor results, just four wins in sixteen matches, Argyle's Vice-Chairman Peter Skinnard revealed that not only was the club looking to bring in new players, but also that the board of directors had committed themselves to well over £200,000 in the club, and of that more than £120,000 came from the Chairman Robert Daniel. Mr Skinnard added that if someone was willing to invest in the club with a total of around £500,000, then both the chairman and he would willingly put any offer to their fellow directors for due consideration.

Dan McCauley and George Gillin have the unique record of having served on all three of Devon's Football League club board of directors. Gillin had a spell as chairman of Exeter City during the club's financially troubled times in the early 1960s, and also served as a director with Torquay United.

McCauley, appointed Plymouth Argyle chairman during the 1991/92 season, had started his 'football directorship' career with Exeter City, until

removed by his fellow board members at St James's Park when he made a bid to take over the club by floating additional shares. He later had a short spell as a director at Torquay United, where his company, Rotolok, sponsored the club's first team strip. Rotolok were to sponsor the Argyle shirts for the 1992/93 season.

Stuart Dawe was chairman of Plymouth Argyle in the 1980s, later joining the Exeter City board of directors in 1991.

DOCKYARD

The City of Plymouth is synonymous with the Royal Naval Dockyard in Devonport, and not surprisingly there are several connections between the yard and the football club. One of the more unusual stories, however, to be reported in the local Press, concerned Plymouth Argyle's Third Round F.A. Cup tie at Home Park against Huddersfield Town in January 1934. It was revealed that many of the dockyard workers finished work early, at lunch time, thus foregoing any lucrative overtime payments. This enabled them to attend Argyle's match in the afternoon. A crowd of 44,500 packed into Home Park and saw Argyle draw 1-1. For the record the replay back at Huddersfield Town resulted in a 6-1 defeat for Plymouth.

The *Western Morning News* reported that for Argyle's match at Southampton in October 1946, an excursion was organised by the Supporters' Club, as well as "another contingent from the Dockyard making the journey". On arriving at The Dell the Plymouth team found a good luck telegram waiting for them in the dressing room from the Westcountry Association of Southampton. Argyle had no luck at all though, crashing to a 5-1 defeat in front of a crowd of twenty four thousand.

It was not at all unusual for coach parties and special train excursions to be organised by Dockyard workers to follow the Plymouth Argyle team away. This particularly applied to the 'big games', such as F.A. Cup ties etc.

Even in the 1920s organised parties of Dockyard workers travelled to Argyle matches. The N.C. Touring Company of Plymouth for instance, ran two charabancs aptly named 'The Argyle' and 'The Argyle Reserve'. Both had a top speed of twelve m.p.h. (five minutes for every mile travelled!). The vehicles were regularly utilised by the fervent Dockyard Argyle supporters to transport them from around the city's environs to Home Park.

Striker Derek Rickard gave up his job in the Dockyard, where he was employed as a joiner, to sign a two year full professional contract with Plymouth Argyle in March 1970. He had been playing as a part time professional for Argyle and was such a success that he was voted Player of the Year for the 1969/70 season. Rickard went on to make nearly 150 appearances for Argyle before moving to A.F.C. Bournemouth for a further two season stay.

DO IT YOURSELF

When full back Moses Russell signed for Plymouth Argyle for a fee of £400 in the summer of 1914 from Merthyr Town, his great friend, centre forward Jack Fowler, who later played for Argyle, volunteered to help decorate Russell's new house in Plymouth and carry out some D.I.Y work. It was reported that after the pair had been busily working all day re-decorating rooms, they suddenly realised that they had in fact moved into the wrong empty house and all their work was wasted! Both players became publicans after retiring from playing, Russell in Plymouth, and Fowler in Swansea.

ELM COTTAGE

Elm Cottage was bought by the club for £20,000 in October 1976 to provide accommodation for apprentices, trialists and schoolboy players. Previously they had stayed in digs throughout the city, but now they could all stay in one place, thus developing good team spirit. The Cottage was situated near the Home Park ground in the south west corner of Pellows Field. A further £10,000 was spent refurbishing the property before it was officially opened. Former Argyle favourite, defender George Robertson, who made 382 appearances for the club between 1951 and 1964, along with his wife June, were appointed to live in Elm Cottage and generally look after the well being of Argyle's young apprentices. There were seven bedrooms enabling a maximum of eighteen youngsters to be accommodated, plus a self-contained flat for the Robertsons. Despite the undoubted success of the

venture, Elm Cottage was sold by the club in the 1980s for financial reasons.

ENTERTAINING

Before the advent of motorways and high speed train links, teams who visited Plymouth Argyle would occasionally stop over on the Saturday night after the game. The Argyle Supporters' Club would then hold a dance where supporters had the chance to meet both the Plymouth and visiting teams players. One such dance held after Argyle's game with West Ham United on February 5th 1948 took place at the Devonport Guildhall. In the match programme it stated: "All dancers are invited to attend between 8 p.m. and 11 p.m., and to meet both teams. Tommy Lawton, that great sportsman, stated that he had never met such a great body of enthusiasts as those at Plymouth, and now you all have an opportunity to prove it to the players of West Ham." The Argyle supporters were no doubt in good heart at the function, for they defeated the Hammers 2-0 with goals from Ray Goddard and George Silk. One wonders what would have happened if the game had been an ill-tempered one?

EUROPEAN CUP WINNERS CUP

The night European club soccer came to Plymouth! Following serious crowd disturbances in the first leg of their first round European Cup Winners Cup match at St Etienne in France, Manchester United were fined £7,500 and ordered to play the second leg at least 300 kilometres away from their Old Trafford ground. United, who had drawn the game 1-1, were thrown out of the competition altogether at first, but after appealing against the decision, they were reinstated.

Plymouth Argyle's board of directors agreed to stage the second leg at Home Park on 5th October 1977. United won the game 2-0 before a trouble free 31,634 attendance, with goals from Steve Coppell and Stuart Pearson. A further thirty thousand watched the game on closed circuit television back at Old Trafford.

The United team that took the field at Home Park will no doubt stir a few memories, and was as follows: Alex Stepney, Jimmy Nicholl, Arthur Albiston, Sammy McIlroy, Brian Greenhoff, Martin Buchan, Steve Coppell, Jimmy Greenhoff, Stuart Pearson, Lou Macari and Gordon Hill. Paul McGrath replaced Pearson during the game.

EXETER CITY

There has always been great rivalry between Plymouth Argyle and the men from up the A38, Exeter City. Despite the fact that Exeter may be the county town of Devon, as far as Plymouth Argyle supporters are concerned, they have the premier football team in the county. This is a fact that cannot be disputed in terms of the respective playing records and status. There has

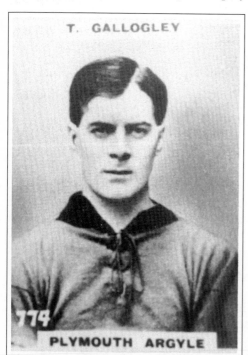

T. GALLOGLEY

PLYMOUTH ARGYLE

never been quite the same passionate rivalry between Argyle and Torquay United, as there has between the two cities of Devon, Plymouth and Exeter.

Needless to say, there are numerous connections between the clubs, with players having been transferred from Plymouth to Exeter, although not so many in the opposite direction. Even managers and directors have switched clubs. Bobby Saxton, in 1979 for instance, left Exeter where he had been team manager and led the club to promotion in 1976/77 for the Plymouth Argyle 'hot seat'. It was something of a homecoming for Saxton though, who had previously made over two hundred League appearances for Argyle between 1968 and 1975.

Players who have made the short journey between the clubs having been transferred from Plymouth Argyle to Exeter City include: Alan Banks

John Delve

(1967), John Banks (1908), Colin Buckingham (1965), Wilf Carter (1964), Peter Darke (1976 on loan), John Delve (1978), Tony Dennis (1983), Crad Evans (1909), George Foster (1981 on loan), Bryce Fulton (1964), Tom Gallogley (1923), Reg Gibson (1947), Ray Goddard (1949), Arthur Greenaway (1950), Alex Hardie (1933), John Hore (1976), Reg Jenkins (1960), Harry Kirk (1922), Charlie Miller (1926), John Mitten (1968), Fred Molyneux (1970 on loan), John Newman (1967), Gordon Nisbet (1987), John Porteous (1956), Colin Randell (1977), Barry Rowan (1970), Darren Rowbotham (1987), Bobby Saxton (1975), Peter Shearing (1968), Kevin Summerfield (1990 on loan), Keith Thomas (1956), Adrian Thorne (1963), William Wake (1908), Jimmy Walker (1926), Bob Wallace (1937), Peter Williams (1960) and George Willis (1956).

Players who have made the move in the opposite direction from Exeter City to Plymouth Argyle include: Alan Banks (1966), Arthur Davies (1935), Crad Evans (1910), Harry Holt (1913), Tony Kellow (1983), Harry Kirk (1922), Nicky Marker (1987), Alf Matthews (1926), Colin Randell (1979), Arthur Rutter (1911), Peter Shearing (1966), John Sims (1979) and Dave Walter (1990).

Tony Kellow

The first occasion Plymouth Argyle met Exeter City in a first team competitive match occurred in a Southern League fixture at St James's Park on Saturday, 11th November 1908, with Exeter winning 2-1 before an attendance of seven thousand. The return match at Home Park, witnessed by eight thousand spectators, was on 10th March 1909 when Argyle ran out easy winners by 4-0.

Since those games, Argyle and City have

crossed each others paths on numerous occasions, and in various competitions. As far as first team competitive games are concerned, Plymouth and Exeter have met each other in the Football League, F.A. Cup, Football League Cup, Associate Members Cup, Southern League, Southern Charity Cup, Spooner Cup, Devon Professional Championship and the Devon Professional Bowl.

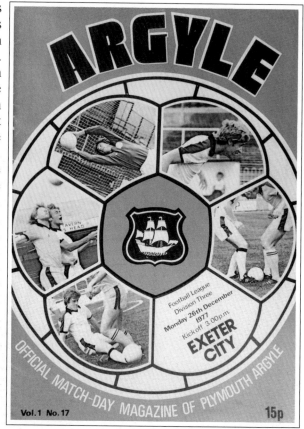

The biggest victory recorded by Argyle over Exeter City was 8-3 in a friendly fixture at St James's Park on 15th March 1911. However the best win in a first team competitive game was a resounding 5-0, again at St James's Park, in a Devon Professional Championship encounter on 9th October 1935.

A unique occasion took place at Torquay United's Plainmoor ground on 15th November 1961, when a combined Torquay and Exeter City team played Plymouth Argyle in a benefit match for United defender Dave Stocks who had to retire from the game through an ankle injury.

When Plymouth Argyle visited Exeter City in August 1977 for the first leg of their Football League Cup tie in the first round, they were literally given the red carpet treatment. The game was sponsored by Exeter's John Holt Carpets who laid a roll of red carpet from the dressing room tunnel out on to the pitch for both teams and the match officials to make a grand entrance.

Argyle defender George Foster spent most of the 1981/82 season on loan at Exeter City, making 28 league appearances for the Grecians. He made such an impression with the St James's Park supporters that Foster was voted Exeter City Player of the Year, despite the fact that by then he had returned to Argyle at the end of his loan period. Foster was player manager of Mansfield Town in 1992/93.

F.A. CUP

Plymouth Argyle's first venture in the F.A. Cup was in 1903. They reached the first round proper after safely negotiating the earlier rounds by defeating Whiteheads (at home) 7-0, Freemantle (home) 5-1, Swindon Town (home) 2-1, and Brentford (home) 4-1 in a replay, after a 1-1 draw at Griffin Park. Over twenty thousand were present at Home Park for the visit of Sheffield Wednesday in the first round proper, and they saw Argyle draw 2-2, with goals from Bob Dalrymple and Jack Peddie. The replay ended any hopes that Plymouth may have had of progressing as they lost 2-0.

Wolverhampton Wanderers paraded the F.A. Cup before the Home Park crowd in January 1950. Wolves had won the 1948/49 final with a 3-1 win over Leicester City at Wembley Stadium. They started their defence of the trophy with a third round visit to Plymouth Argyle, and before the kick off

the Wolves team walked around the Home Park pitch proudly showing the F.A. Cup to the forty thousand crowd, the trophy being carried securely strapped on a stretcher by two St John Ambulance Brigade members! The game ended all square at one goal apiece, with South African Stan Williams netting for Plymouth. Wolves won the replay back at Molyneux 3-0.

Cup fever well and truly arrived in the 1983/84 season, when Argyle progressed all the way to the semi-final stage of the F.A. Cup, this being the best run in the club's history. It was not all straightforward, however, with two tricky replays having to be negotiated in earlier rounds.

Argyle drew 0-0 at Southend United in the first round, winning the replay back at Home Park 2-0 after extra-time, with goals from the irrepressible Tommy Tynan, and a Micky Stead own goal. Round two saw non-leaguers Barking of the Isthmian League come to Plymouth and, after a not very convincing performance by Argyle, they edged through to the third round winning 2-1, with goals from diminutive midfielder Mark Rowe and defender Lindsay Smith.

The expected 'big club' in the third round turned out to be Newport County! The Welshmen proved to be a tough nut to crack though, and the tie at Home Park ended all square at two goals a piece. A Kevin Hodges goal and an injury time penalty from Tommy Tynan saved Plymouth's blushes. Argyle travelled to Somerton Park for the replay and a Andy Rogers goal proved to be enough to win the game.

Round four and another unfashionable club, this time a first ever meeting with Fourth Division Darlington. Again Plymouth were far from convincing, but nevertheless they still won, 2-1 with John Uzzell and Gordon Staniforth being the scorers.

Now it was on to the last sixteen teams left in the competition. An away draw at West Bromwich Albion which prompted Argyle to give their best performance of the Cup run so far, and a 1-0 victory thanks to another Tommy Tynan goal. By now cup fever had well and truly arrived, and an attendance of 34,365 witnessed a goalless draw at Home Park against Derby County in the quarter-final. The match produced club record receipts of

23

£118,000. The odds were stacked against Argyle in the replay, however, but a fighting display and a goal from Andy Rogers netting direct from a corner kick kept Plymouth's Wembley dream alive.

The days leading up to the semi-final really had the Plymouth and surrounding area, and indeed the whole of Devon and Cornwall, buzzing with expectation. Long lost Argyle fans suddenly re-appeared. Could Argyle make it to the shrine of football at Wembley Stadium? A Cup Final appearance? Something which seemed impossible back in that first round at Southend United a few months earlier. The semi-final took place at Villa Park against Watford on 14th April 1984, before an attendance of 43,858, with twenty thousand of those shouting on the Argyle. The two teams on this memorable and historic occasion, as far as Argyle were concerned, lined up as follows:

PLYMOUTH ARGYLE: Geoff Crudgington, Gordon Nisbet, John Uzzell, Chris Harrison, Lindsay Smith, Leigh Cooper, Kevin Hodges, David Phillips, Tommy Tynan, Gordon Staniforth, Andy Rogers.

WATFORD: Steve Sherwood, David Bardsley, Neil Price, Les Taylor, Steve Terry (Richard Jobson), Lee Sinnott, Nigel Callaghan, Maurice Johnston, George Reilly, Wilf Rostron, John Barnes.

Action from the F.A. Cup Semi Final Argyle v. Watford at Villa Park, 14th April 1984.

25

Alas, the Wembley dream evaporated in the 'unlucky for Plymouth' thirteenth minute, when a piece of John Barnes wizardry took him past Gordon Nisbet, and he sent over a cross of deadly accuracy for the tall George Reilly to head past Geoff Crudgington. Plymouth put up a gallant fight to conjure an equaliser, but the task was just too much for the Third Division club. It was not to be Argyle's day. It was however ninety minutes of football that everyone who was present will remember for evermore. The Cup run had ended, but Plymouth Argyle Football Club had really put their name firmly on the map!

Agyle's Cup dreams are shattered as George Reilly heads home John Barnes's cross to give Watford victory.

The second round tie between Plymouth Argyle and non-league Barking in December 1983 almost did not take place because of a strike! The Barking players threatened to withdraw their services following a dispute between the club and manager Peter Carey. The manager left, and the players were so incensed that they were prepared not to fulfil the cup tie at Home Park. They were eventually persuaded to travel to Devon, and the tie went ahead. Isthmian League Barking did not make it easy for Argyle who struggled to win 2-1.

Plymouth Argyle won three times in F.A. Cup matches as a non-league club against Football League opposition. They defeated Barnsley 1-0 in 1907/08, Preston North End 2-0 in 1912/13, and Lincoln City 4-1 in the following season.

FINANCE

All Football Clubs have financial problems at some stage or another in their history, and Plymouth Argyle are no different to many others in that respect. Indeed during the 1910 close season finances were so poor that a liquidator was actually appointed. Argyle had announced a loss of around

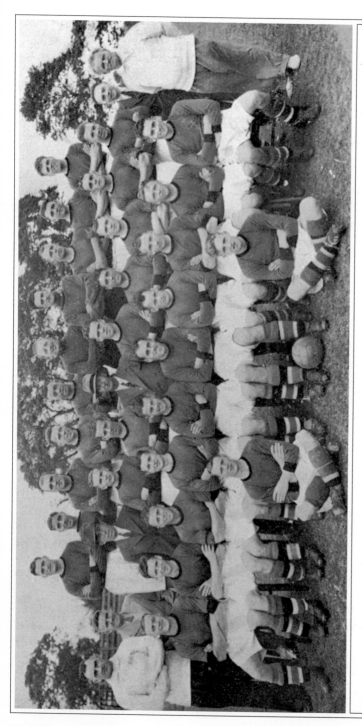

Plymouth Argyle 1937/38. Back row (L to R) F. Toothill, F. Hunter, J. Murray, J. Connor, H. Roberts, T. Foley, H. Cann, T. Black, A. Dyer, S. Kirkwood. Middle row (L to R) W. Harper (Trainer), F. Axworthy, D. Robbie. J. Girvan, T. Ryan, R. Jack (Sec. Manager), T. McColgan, F. Mitcheson, H. Brown, V. Wright, J. McNeil, Dr Cameron, A. Day (Asst Trainer). Front Row (L to R) A. Gorman, T. Dougan, J. Smith, M. Dickie, J. McHarg, J. C. Rae, S. Black, J. Vidler, F. Prescott, M. Morgan. Front (L) J. Mailey, (R) J. Wharton.

£6,000 for the 1909/10 season, and at one stage there were insufficient funds to meet the players' wages. The playing staff did eventually get their money, or at least some of it, when Argyle played a few friendly matches at Home Park, and all the receipts were given to the unpaid players.

Argyle struggled on, but at a shareholders' meeting held in May 1910, it was decided that drastic action was called for, and a liquidator be appointed. This took place a couple of weeks later, but then the following month it was announced that a 'substantial' sum of cash had been injected by the board of directors, notably from Clarence and Stanley Spooner. This ensured that Plymouth Argyle Football Club could continue, staving off any threats of possible closure.

Despite the fact that no competitive professional football was played at Home Park between 1915 and 1919 because of the First World War, it was reported that Plymouth Argyle managed to record a trading profit of £2,824 at the end of the 1919/20 season. This was partly due to the fact that admission charges to first team games had been increased.

During the 1928/29 season, it was reported that Plymouth Argyle's part time professional players were being paid a £1 per week, plus a ten shillings (50p!) win bonus.

At the start of the 1929/30 season it was stated that Plymouth Argyle Football Club had debts of £6,000. However, the club went on to win promotion to the Second Division at the end of the campaign and no doubt dispelled any lingering financial worries.

In 1935 Plymouth Argyle manager Bob Jack had the unpleasant task of informing the staff that the directors were struggling to find the money to pay their wages. The club survived, but were forced to release a few of their professionals in an effort to reduce escalating costs.

The depression years of the 1930s resulted in hard times for Plymouth Argyle. They struggled financially, and the entire board of directors resigned. Once again a crisis was facing the club. An appeal was made to local businessmen to form a new board of directors to keep the club alive and to ease the financial burden of running the club. This proved to be very successful, and at one stage there were no fewer than fifteen directors of the club under the chairmanship of Lieutenant Colonel T. McCready. These gentlemen revived the club's ailing finances by substantially increasing the capital of the company.

Outspoken Plymouth Argyle chairman Ron Blindell promised his players each a £500 bonus if they won promotion to the First Division at the end of the 1960/61 season. He also declared that his players would be paid £30 per week the following season in the higher division. Plymouth in fact ended the 1960/61 season in eleventh position, so no bonus!

The Plymouth Argyle board of directors reported to the annual meeting of shareholders in 1968 that the club had made a record trading loss of

£45,000 on the previous financial year. By the end of the 1969/70 season, Argyle were reported to be £100,000 in debt.

In February 1978 Vice chairman Peter Skinnard revealed that it cost approximately £7,500 per week all the year round to run Plymouth Argyle.

FIRE

A lighted match thrown on to the wooden floor was believed to have been the cause of a fire in the grandstand at Home Park during the second half of the Division Three South encounter with Aberdare Athletic in September 1925. Part of the floor was set ablaze at the back of the stand, but it was quickly dealt with by buckets of water before a much more serious incident occurred. There was just as much action on the field as off it, for Argyle ran out 7-2 winners over their Welsh visitors! The Aberdare club were to lose their Football League status at the end of the following season when they finished bottom of the Third Division South table. Aberdare played in the unusual strip of dark blue and old gold striped shirts and white shorts.

Plymouth Argyle goalkeeper Geoff Crudgington had a memorable afternoon for all the wrong reasons in February 1983. Shortly before setting out for Home Park for the game against Bradford City, Crudgington had to deal with a fire at his house in Plymouth after a pan of fat had caught alight. In putting the fire out, Crudgington suffered burns to his back and waist. Despite the pain, and being treated by the club doctor for the burns right up until kick off, he decided to play in the game. The day ended happily for Crudgington and Plymouth Argyle, as they defeated Bradford City 3-1. Crudgington was still playing and managing Jewson South Western Leaguers, Millbrook, during the 1991/92 season.

FIRSTS

The first professional players to be signed by Plymouth Argyle in 1903 were Robert Jack and Jack Fitchett. The signings took place at the Grand Hotel, Manchester, with Argyle director John Spooner travelling North to meet the two players. Robert Jack had been playing with Glossop, then a Football League Second Division side. Fitchett, who later became manager of the Palace Theatre in Plymouth and had been a team mate of Jack at Bolton Wanderers, had appeared for Southampton in the 1902/03 season.

The club's first competitive match as a professional team took place at West Ham United on September 1st 1903. This was a Western League fixture, with many London area clubs then playing in the competition, which was vastly different from that of today's league. Centre forward, Jack Peddie, had the honour of scoring the first and only goal of the game for Argyle. The team that took to the field was as follows: Jack Robinson, Jack Fitchett, Charlie Clark, Billy Leech, Archie Goodall, Harry Digweed, Bob Dalrymple, Wattie Anderson, Jack Peddie, Jack Picken, Robert Jack.

Four days later Plymouth Argyle, who also played in the Southern

Plymouth Argyle 1903/04 Season. Back row (L to R) W. Anderson, H. Winterholder, C. Clark, F. Fitchett, J. Robinson, A. Clark, J. Banks, J. Picken, B. Jack. Front row (L to R) T. Cleghorn, B. Dalrymple, W. Leech, A. Goodhall, H. Digweed, F. Brettell.

League, played their first match in that competition when they entertained Northampton Town at Home Park. Once again Argyle were successful, before an attendance of 4,438. They won 2-0, with Jack Peddie finding the target along with Jack Picken.

Plymouth Argyle Goalkeeper Jack Robinson holds the unusual distinction of playing for one club in their inaugural Football League season (the now defunct Second Division New Brighton Tower club in 1898/99), and two clubs in their inaugural season of Southern League football (Plymouth Argyle 1903/04 and Exeter City 1908/09).

Luton Town's first game at their Kenilworth Road ground was against Plymouth Argyle in a Southern League fixture on Monday, 4th September 1905. The match ended in a goalless draw.

Argyle also had the honour of being the first team to visit Norwich City's old ground, at The Nest in Rosary Road, for a Football League fixture. The Third Division encounter took place on 4th September 1920, and ended in a 1-1 draw.

Plymouth Argyle's eagerly awaited debut match in the Football League took place on Saturday, 28th August 1920, when Norwich City were the visitors to Home Park. An excited attendance of 17,500 saw Jimmy Heeps head Argyle into a thirtieth-minute lead, but Norwich equalised forty minutes later through Laxton. The Plymouth line up on that historic afternoon was: Fred Craig, Moses Russell, Sep Atterbury, Jim Logan, Jimmy Dickinson, Billy Forbes, Jimmy Kirkpatrick, David Jack, Bertie Bowler, Jimmy Heeps, William Dixon.

The first Plymouth Argyle player to score more than twenty goals in a season in Football League matches was Frank Richardson. Following Argyle's dismal previous season, when the entire team only netted 33 league goals between them, Richardson more than made up for that in 1921/22 with 31 goals in 41 appearances.

The first groundsman at Home Park in 1901 was a Mr W. Tomlinson. The Tomlinson family connection continued at Plymouth Argyle for his son, Harry, was a valuable and long serving member of the office staff for fifty years until retiring in the 1950s.

FISHY TALES

Argyle players Brian Johnson and George Foster liked nothing better than going off on a fishing expedition when not playing or training. The River Yealm was their favourite spot. One summer's afternoon in 1977, however, the pair of them had a very embarrassing experience. The so called 'angling experts' decided to venture into Cornwall and Carlyon Bay for a spot of fishing, taking their wives along. After no luck at all and nothing caught, the ladies decided to have a go. Imagine the players' surprise then when the two 'amateur' ladies then caught a couple of dozen fish in half an hour!

Brian Johnson

FLOODLIGHTS

The first set of floodlights installed at Home Park were officially 'switched-on' in a friendly match against Devon rivals Exeter City on 26th October 1953. The match was played in a near gale and pouring rain which kept the attendance down to just 2,050. Argyle quickly raced into a 2-0 lead with goals from Maurice Tadman (14th minute), and Sam McCrory (15th minute). Angus Mackay pulled a goal back for Exeter, before Malcolm Davies netted a third goal for Argyle in the second half.

During the previous season Plymouth Argyle had travelled to Exeter to play in the first match under floodlights at St James's Park. This was dogged by adverse weather as well, for the original game was due to be played on Tuesday, 3rd March 1953, but it was called off less than an hour before kick-off when fog enveloped the ground. The Argyle party of directors and players were, however, entertained by Exeter City club officials at a dinner, when Plymouth director Edgar Dobell said: "I am sure floodlit football is here to stay. Whilst it is still a novelty, I have little doubt that like a beard it will be sure to grow."

Exeter City and Plymouth Argyle tried again six days later, and this time the game went ahead successfully before an attendance of 8,130, Argyle winning 3-0 with goals from Eric Davis, Harold Dobbie and Neil Dougall.

Much more recently, Plymouth Argyle played in another inaugural floodlit match, this time at Great Mills League Torrington. The friendly fixture took place in October 1988 against the North Devon side managed by the former Plymouth boss John Hore, who had been in charge when the men from Home Park had reached the semi-final of the F.A. Cup four years previously. Hore was still managing Torrington in 1992/93.

FOOTBALL LEAGUE CUP

The Football League Cup competition started in the 1960/61 season, and Plymouth Argyle's first opponents were Southport at Home Park. Goals from Jimmy McAnearney and Alex Jackson gave Plymouth a 2-0 win. Argyle went on to reach round four before losing at home to the eventual cup winners, Aston Villa 5-3.

Plymouth Argyle have reached the semi-final stage of the Football League Cup on two occasions in 1964/65, and 1973/74. On the first occasion they lost to Leicester City 4-2 on aggregate. In 1973/74 Manchester City ended Plymouth's dreams of a final appearance, by drawing 1-1 on a gluepot of a pitch at Home Park before 30,390 spectators, and then winning 2-0 back at Maine Road in the second leg.

GOALS

Plymouth Argyle became the first Third Division South club to reach a century of goals in a season. They netted 107 goals in 1925/26, when Argyle were runners up to Reading. The previous record for goals scored in the Third Division South, which had only been formed in 1921, was held by Portsmouth with 87 goals in the 1923/24 season.

The total of 107 goals is a club record for League goals scored in a single season. This has been achieved on two occasions, in 1925/26 and 1951/52. The men who were on target in 1925/26 were Jack Cock 31 goals, Sammy Black 19, Jack Leslie 17, Fred Forbes 14, Patsy Corcoran 6, Alf Mathews 5, Jimmy Logan 4, Fred McKenzie 3, Jimmy Healey 2, John Pullen 2, Bert Batten 2 and Frank Sloan 1, plus two own goals – Jenkins (Brighton & Hove Albion) and Smith (Newport County).

The 1951/52 goalgetters were Maurice Tadman 27, George Dews 25, Peter Rattray 19, Gordon Astall 18, Alex Govan 9, Neil Dougall 3, Paddy Ratcliffe 3, Jack Chisholm 1 and Bill Strauss 1, plus one own goal – Russon (Walsall).

Jack Fowler dented proud Pompey's magnificent start to the 1922/23

The high scoring, promotion-winning, Argyle team 1951/52 lined up as follows: Back row (L to R) W. Strauss, A. McShane, W. Shortt, G. Taylor, A. Polkinghorne, L. Major, J. Chisholm, L. Ball, W. Adams, P. Langman, J. Smith. Middle row (L to R) Mr G. Hackworthy, G. Silk, S. Dixon, A. Machin, L. Jelly, P. Jones, G. Robertson, J. Sim, J. Porteous, S. Rundle, P. Anderson, S. Wyatt, N. Roberts, R. Tilley, G. Reed (Trainer). Front row (L to R) P. Ratcliffe, G. Astall, P. Rattray, G. Willis, G. Dews, M. Tadman, N. Dougall, A. Govan, H. Dobbie, L. Kneebone, Short, Sweeney.

Legendary goalscorer Tommy Tynan scores the first of his four goals against Blackburn Rovers at Home Park.

season. The Plymouth Argyle forward became the first player to score against Portsmouth that season, the South coast club having not conceded a goal in their previous eight matches. Fowler's first minute goal helped Argyle to a 2-1 win, Bert Batten also being on target for the visitors.

Centre forward Percy Cherrett achieved a remarkable run of goalscoring form for Plymouth Argyle during the 1923/24 season. After scoring for Argyle at Queens Park Rangers on 1st December 1923, he then proceeded to score two goals in each of the next five league fixtures, against Queens Park Rangers (at home), Newport County (home and away), and Exeter City (home and away). His superb record ended in a 1-1 draw at home to Merthyr Town on 29th December. Cherrett had played eight matches in the month of December and scored eleven goals!

Dave Thomas scored in each of an amazing ten consecutive Second Division fixtures for Plymouth Argyle during the 1946/47 season. He netted in a 4-1 defeat at Chesterfield on New Year's Day, and then went on to score in successive games versus Sheffield Wednesday, Fulham, Bury, Luton Town, Leicester City, Southampton, Barnsley, Burnley, ending his

The Argyle team of 1966/67 which features Mike Bickle, the goal-scoring milkman, fourth from right at the back and Alan Banks, third from left in the third row.

goalscoring run against Tottenham Hotspur on 29th March 1947. Thomas scored one goal in each of the matches apart from the encounter with Luton, when he registered a double. Thomas had his career at Argyle, like so many others, interrupted by the war years, having been signed in 1938 from Romford.

Millwall suffered their record Football League defeat at Home Park on 16th January 1932, when Plymouth Argyle triumphed 8-1 before an attendance of 15,799. Jack Vidler scored a hat-trick, the other Argyle goalscorers being Ray Bowden 2, Sammy Black, Jack Leslie, and an own goal from Millwall's Pipe.

Plymouth Argyle have been involved in some amazing matches over the Christmas period, notably in 1955 against Bristol City, and five years later versus Charlton Athletic. The goals flowed as liberally as the Christmas spirit (alcohol version that is!). Bristol City visited Home Park in a Second Division fixture on Boxing Day 1955, and were comprehensively beaten 5-0 before 22,096 spectators. The Argyle goalgetters were Jimmy Crawford 2, Malcolm Davies, Eric Davis, and Johnny Williams. But 24 hours later in the return fixture at Ashton Gate it was Plymouth's turn to suffer, as they crashed to a 6-0 beating!

The Christmas games against Charlton Athletic in 1960 were even more unpredictable, with a few more goals as well! In the Boxing Day fixture at the Valley, Argyle slipped to a 6-4 defeat, with George Kirby scoring twice, and a goal each for Peter Anderson and John Williams. The very next day at Home Park, Plymouth turned the tables and scoreline in their favour by defeating Charlton by 6-4! The odds of that happening must have been astronomical. Over twenty three thousand fans saw Wilf Carter net five

This picture of the Plymouth Argyle team of 1960/61 features Wilf Carter on the left of the back row; beside him (L to R) D. Roberts, C. Buckingham, G. Barnsley, D. Maclaren, G. Fincham, R. Smith, J. Leiper, M. Reeves, R. Davis. Middle row (L to R) C. Dougall (Coach), R. Jenkins, T. Stacey, G. Robertson, W. Wright, K. Maloy, A. Jackson, B. Fulton, L. Casey, P. Kearns, M. Waterfield, R. Wyatt, J. L. Williams, G. Taylor (Trainer). Front row (L to R) J. MacAnearney, G. Kirby, J. Newman, P. W. Skinnard, R. J. R. Blindell (Chairman), Lt Col R. V. Hunt, J. W. Hall, J. S. Williams, T. Dann, P. Anderson. Front (L) G. Howshall (R) A. Rounsevell.

times, with Alex Jackson adding the other goal. Charlton's Dennis Edwards also had good reason to remember those two games, for he scored two in each encounter!

Sixteen-year-old apprentice professional Richard Reynolds scored nine goals in Plymouth Argyle's win over their hapless Cornish opponents Bugle in a South Western League fixture in January 1965. He then found himself thrust into first team football just three days later in a third round F.A. Cup tie at Home Park against Derby County. Although Reynolds didn't score, he nevertheless assisted Argyle to a 4-2 win.

Frank Richardson made a sensational start to his Football League career with Plymouth Argyle. Having been signed from non-league side Barking Town, centre forward Richardson lined up for his debut for the club at Bristol Rovers in August 1921, and promptly netted a hat-trick as Plymouth won 3-1. Richardson scored 37 goals in 63 league appearances for Argyle before moving to Stoke City in 1923.

HARPER'S PARK

Plymouth Argyle's training ground was named after Bill Harper who gave such sterling service to the club in various capacities over a long period of time spanning nearly fifty years. He started his playing career at Hibernians and then played for Arsenal, winning eleven Scottish International caps. Harper moved to Plymouth Argyle in 1931, going on to make 75 appearances before retiring from playing. He then began his 'backroom' career with the club and was appointed Argyle's trainer in 1935, after five years becoming groundsman and later kit manager. Harper enjoyed a well-earned testimonial match in 1972/73 when Plymouth Argyle played against Arsenal to reward his marvellous service to the club.

Bill Harper

HAT-TRICKS

Frank Richardson netted three hat-tricks for Plymouth Argyle in the 1921/22 season. These came against Bristol Rovers, Swansea Town and Brentford, all the games being played at Home Park.

The first ever Football League hat-trick by an Argyle player away from home was scored by Jack Cock in a 4-1 win at Watford in February 1927.

The first F.A. Cup hat-trick notched by an Argyle player was in a 4-1 win at home to Bradford Park Avenue in February 1923, the honour going to that prolific scorer Frank Richardson.

Frank Lord became the first Argyle player to score a hat-trick in the Football League Cup, during a fourth round replay against Stoke City at Home Park in November 1964, Plymouth winning the tie 3-1.

Notts County's Albert Keetley netted a hat-trick against Plymouth Argyle in the Second Division match at Home Park on 10th October 1931. Argyle lost 4-3, and it was the start of a remarkable sequence for the County goalgetter. Keetley went on to score hat-trick in each of the two following games, against Manchester United and Chesterfield!

HOME PARK

The Home Park ground was originally the headquarters of the now long-defunct Devonport Albion Rugby Club. They were, however, involved in a rent dispute with their landlords, and the ground remained unoccupied for three years until the Argyle Athletic Club moved there. The first sporting event staged at Home Park after Mr Clarence Spooner obtained the lease at Whitsun 1901 was an athletics meeting. The approaches to the ground were somewhat different than they are now though, for a glimpse at an old city map of the area reveals that supporters had to trudge along a pathway and a lane from the Pennycomequick roundabout, across the fields, and even over a stile! Supporters could stop and look at the adjoining farm and animals grazing. From those early days, Home Park has evolved into the ground we all know today.

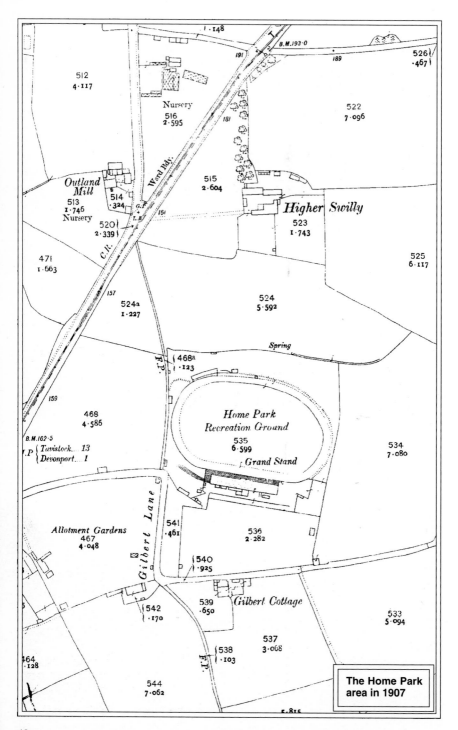

The Home Park
area in 1907

40

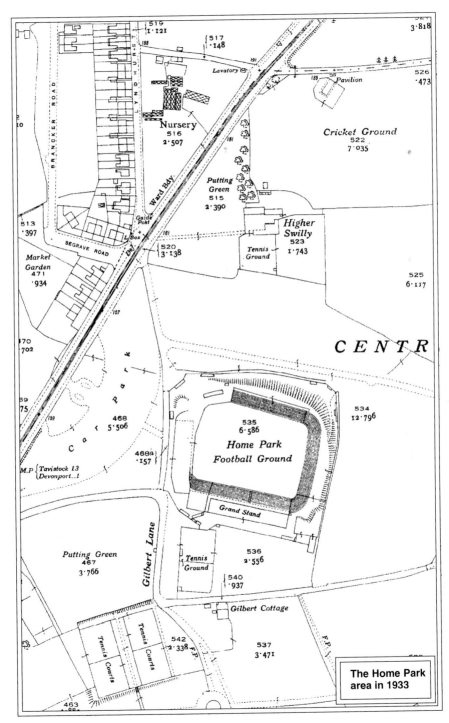

The Home Park area in 1933

41

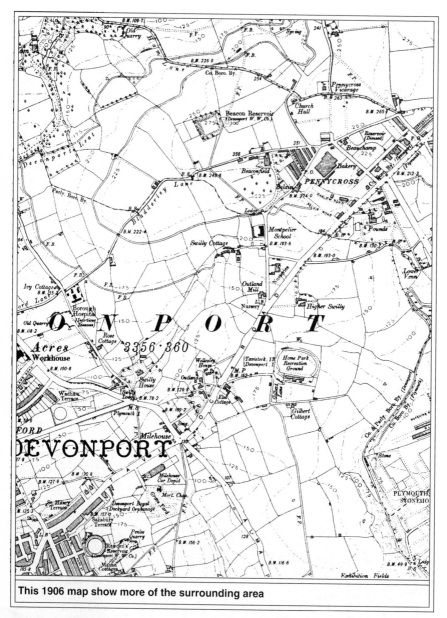

This 1906 map show more of the surrounding area

1901: The ground consisted of open standing, the banking being constructed of slag heaps. There was however a small wooden grandstand which stretched about forty yards or so, with a pointed gable roof, and stood roughly on the site of the present one. Dressing rooms could be found under this structure. There was also a stand opposite known as 'The Flowerpot

Stand' or the 'Spooner Stand' as it sported a large advertisement for Clarence Spooner's store in the city! A wooden fence separated spectators from the playing area. Various sporting events were then staged at Home Park, not only football, but also pony trotting and whippet racing!

1903: Plymouth Argyle rented Home Park from the Argyle Athletic Club for the sum of £300 for the first season of professional football in the city.

1905: Home Park was described as being "one of the best and prettiest grounds in the South of England. It can accommodate twenty five thousand spectators and is capable of unlimited expansion."

1930: The car park outside the ground was used for the first time for Argyle's Second Division fixture with relegated Everton on 30th August 1930. It was estimated that some 1,200 cars from all over the Westcountry packed the new site, with a crowd of 34,916 present to witness Argyle lose 3-2.

The original, and by then inadequate, wooden grandstand was demolished, although Argyle did earn themselves a few 'pennies' by selling the timber.

A more modern and much bigger structure, stretching the length of the pitch, was built at a cost of £11,000. The hard working Plymouth Argyle Supporters' Club paid for the roofing of the Devonport end which cost £1,500.

1932: The roofing of the Devonport end was extended to join up with the grandstand roof.

1936: A new main entrance to the ground was constructed, again paid for by the valuable donations from the Supporters' Club.

1941: The Football Club did not go unscathed in the Second World War, indeed during the blitz in 1941 the Home Park ground sustained extensive

damage. The impressive eleven-year-old grandstand, including the offices and dressing rooms, was reduced to rubble, and the pitch was left full of craters. Unfortunately there was a lot of household furniture stored under the grandstand for safe keeping by families living nearby Home Park, who had suffered in earlier raids.

1945: Football resumed, but such was the devastation of Home Park that players changed for games in huts and even corporation double-decker buses, which were utilised for temporary accommodation. The site of the destroyed grandstand was tidied up a little by laying old wooden railway sleepers which became a form of rudimentary terracing. Temporary uncovered seating was also installed. The large craters in the playing surface were filled with rubble from other bomb damaged sites in the city. It was a massive task to get Home Park ready to stage football again.

The Plymouth Argyle and visiting club directors were catered for by the building of a wooden pavilion, converted from two army huts, built on girders high above the corner of the ground at the Barn Park end to the right of the destroyed main grandstand.

1948: The only cover for spectators at this time was found at the Devonport end, there was no grandstand, Home Park consisting of 'open' terracing on three sides of the ground. The Argyle directors made an application to build a 2,500-seater grandstand to replace the one destroyed during the war. It was estimated that the structure would cost £20,000 to build. However, the application was refused by the Ministry of Works as they could only give their approval at that time to projects which were designed to prevent danger to the public.

1952: Grandstand 'number three', the present one, known as the Mayflower Stand, was built and used for the first time. Construction on the rebuilding of the grandstand had started a year earlier.

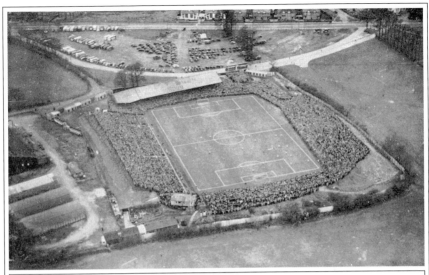

This aerial view shows Home Park as it looked at the beginning of 1948.

1953: Floodlights were installed, and officially 'switched on' in a friendly against neighbouring Exeter City.

1964: The terracing on the Lyndhurst side of the ground (opposite the grandstand) was roofed over.

1969: The grandstand was reseated to bring its capacity up to just over four thousand.

1977: The Devonport end terrace roofing was removed. It was by then 47 years old and was deemed to be unsafe. Argyle had no alternative but to dismantle it as they could not at the time afford to replace it. Unfortunately, it was the end of the ground that the club's most vociferous supporters normally congregated, with the noise they generated echoing off the roof, but once this was removed, the ground lost some of its atmosphere.

1979: An all weather training pitch was constructed and opened in association with the Sports Council. Situated behind the main grandstand, facilities included a floodlit play area, and changing accommodation. Local groups of youngsters were also encouraged to use the pitch with Argyle coaching staff being in attendance.

1984: A new roof, although covering a smaller area, to replace the one which had been removed seven years earlier, was erected over the Devonport end at a cost of £40,000.

1986: Sixteen Executive Boxes installed at the rear of the grandstand.

Between February 1986 and February 1989 a sum total of £720,000 was spent at Home Park carrying out various safety features and general improvements, following the implementation of safety reports into sports

grounds. This included work on the terraces, changing rooms, police surveillance facilities, and hospitality areas. The old directors' pavilion dating from 1945, was taken over for use by the Police. Work also took place on the roof of the popular side of the ground, relaying terraces at Barn Park and Devonport ends, and in Mayflower enclosure. New baths and showers were provided for the players. The Lyndhurst side of the ground was later made an all-seated enclosure.

Life-long supporter Sam Rendell at Home Park in October 1992.

HOSTILITIES

Competitive football ended for Plymouth Argyle in 1915, when the club was closed for the duration of the First World War. Games involving service personnel did take place at Home Park, but it was not until 1919/20 that Argyle were able to resume their Southern League fixtures.

Inside forward Bert Bowler, who was serving with the Sherwood Foresters, made an appearance for England in an unofficial international fixture against Scotland in Cairo during the First World War. Bowler was to join Plymouth Argyle after the War and make over a hundred appearances for the club before retiring in 1923.

The 1939/40 season came to an abrupt halt after just three games were played, the war effort taking obvious priority. At the time Plymouth Argyle had won two of their games and lost the other, scoring four goals and conceding three. Top of Division One to Four at that time were Blackpool, Reading, Luton Town and Accrington Stanley respectively. Football was then re-organised into regional divisions for the duration of the war years.

Money and players were both in short supply during wartime football. In 1939/40 for instance, Plymouth Argyle agreed to play Newport County in the South West Regional League on consecutive days, giving up home advantage. Argyle had agreed to switch their home fixture with Newport to Somerton Park so that the Welsh club could save on travelling expenses, Argyle's 'home' fixture thus being played in Wales. Plymouth went on to become South West Regional League Champions that season, with neighbouring Torquay United finishing as runners-up. The League incidentally consisted of Bristol City, Bristol Rovers, Cardiff City, Newport County, Swansea Town, Swindon Town, Torquay United and the Argyle. Exeter City were not included as the club decided to temporarily 'close down' during the war period, and their ground was taken over for military use by the locally stationed American Forces.

Argyle made a brief appearance in the Wartime League Cup, being defeated 5-1 at Home Park in the very first round by Bournemouth and Boscombe Athletic.

The footballing activities of Plymouth Argyle were suspended at the end of the 1939/40 season and did not resume until 1945/46. Plymouth, being a strategic naval city, sustained substantial damage from bombing, with the Home Park ground being hit on several occasions.

Former Welsh International, Birmingham City and Cardiff City winger George Edwards, recalls playing a match for Birmingham at Home Park in the 1945/46 season. Because of the bombing there were no grandstands, and no dressing rooms, the players having to change in corrugated tin huts. He also remembers that players had the 'luxury' of buckets of water, instead of baths, after the game.

Not surprisingly the 1945/46 season proved to be something of a disaster as far as Plymouth Argyle were concerned in the re-organised and temporary South League. With rudimentary arrangements at the ground, and a number of players unavailable, they had to rely heavily on guest players to make up the numbers. Players travelled from all over the country to appear in the Argyle team, and even as far away as Scotland. Consequently they never achieved a settled line up, and used no fewer than seventy two different players to complete their 42 League South fixtures. Argyle finished bottom of the league with the following playing record: Played 42, Won 3, Drew 8, Lost 31, For 39 Against 120, Points 14. Birmingham City were to win the League Championship, with Aston Villa finishing as runners-up.

Argyle didn't fare any better in the F.A. Cup that season either, being eliminated by Aldershot in the Third Round. Plymouth were exempt until that stage of the competition, but after losing 2-0 at Aldershot in the first leg, also went down 1-0 back at Home Park in the return match.

Argyle manager Jack Tresadern wrote to the Football League asking them for permission to stage a special game to take place against Bristol City on 24th August 1946 at Home Park. As both clubs had suffered greatly during the blitz, having had their respective grandstands destroyed, it was suggested that the clubs could share any gate receipts, less the entertainment tax levied, to use solely on rebuilding facilities. The League agreed to Argyle's request, with Bristol City winning 6-3 before an attendance of 16,998 which produced gate receipts of £973 8s 3d.

INTERNATIONAL AND REPRESENTATIVE MATCHES

The Football League representative side, containing seven of the England World Cup winning squad, played the Irish League at Home Park in September 1966. The hapless Irish side were simply overrun, losing 12-0 before an appreciative Westcountry crowd of 35,458. That talented Football League team is well worth recalling. They were: Peter Bonetti (Chelsea), George Cohen (Fulham), Ray Wilson (Everton), Martin Peters (West Ham United), Jackie Charlton (Leeds United), Bobby Moore (West Ham United), Terry Paine (Southampton), Johnny Byrne (West Ham United), George Eastham (Stoke City) and John Connelly (Blackburn Rovers). The substitute on this big occasion was Plymouth Argyle's John Newman.

Three under-23 International matches have been staged at Home Park. The first took place in November 1962 when England defeated Belgium 6-1. The England goalscorers were Martin Peters 2, Mike O'Grady, Derek Stokes, Alan Suddick and Bobby Tambling.

The second under-23 fixture was played in April 1970 between England and Bulgaria. Plymouth Argyle Chairman Robert Daniel said: "It is a privilege for Plymouth Argyle to stage an important international. Westcountry fans have shown before that they will respond eagerly to the chance of seeing top class soccer and we, as a club, are delighted to have the opportunity of staging this match. It is gratifying to know that our fine ground and facilities are appreciated."

To add to the occasion, Argyle's talented Norman Piper won his first under-23 cap and helped England to a 4-1 win before an attendance of 28,056.

The third match saw England take on Portugal in October 1973, a goalless draw being the outcome.

An under-21 European Championship International between England and Poland was played at Home Park in June 1989, with England winning 2-1.

The England Youth team have also staged their International fixtures at Plymouth Argyle's ground. These have been against Denmark (1955 – England winning 9-2!) and Wales (1952).

England Amateur International matches have been played at Home Park on at least three occasions with the opponents being Wales (1914 and 1925) and Italy (1972). A member of the England 1914 team to grace Home Park, was Plymouth Argyle player, Harry Raymond, who had joined the club five years earlier from local Plymouth and District League side, Woodland Villa.

IRON CURTAIN

An adventurous tour, before the spirit of Glasnost in the 1990s, to the two Iron Curtain countries of East Germany and Poland was undertaken by Plymouth Argyle in May 1963. The playing squad for the four match tour consisted of Stuart Brace, Colin Buckingham, Wilf Carter, Richard Davis, John Leiper, Jimmy McAnearney, Dave MacLaren, Johnny Newman, Alan O'Neill, Peter McParland, Mike Reeves, Dave Roberts, George Robertson, Mike Trebilcock and Johnny Williams.

The first match was in Warsaw against the Polish Army team, Warsaw Legia. An astounding one hundred thousand spectators, the biggest crowd that Argyle have ever played in front of, saw Legia narrowly win 2-1, Wilf Carter netting the Argyle goal.

Two days later the Plymouth team made a coach journey to Poznan, where they lost 1-0 to K.S.C. Lech before fifty thousand spectators. The match had an unusual start, for the matchball was delivered by helicopter, being dropped on to the pitch!

The shipbuilding area of Gdansk was the next stop of the tour. Argyle's opponents were B.W.K.S. Lechia, and the sixty thousand crowd saw the Devonian team win 3-0. The goalscorers were Wilf Carter, Jimmy McAnearney and Alan O'Neill.

After bidding their Polish hosts farewell, it was off to Erfurt in the former East Germany for the final game against S.C. Turbine. Played in a heatwave, the game was an exciting one, with the East Germans winning narrowly 3-2. Another good crowd of forty thousand were present to see Peter McParland and Mike Trebilcock get the Argyle goals.

JUGGLING

Argyle inside forward Dave Burnside had a well known reputation for giving pre-match displays of ball juggling. This began at his first professional club, West Bromwich Albion, when he would tap the ball around from foot, to head, to knee, and balanced it on various parts of his anatomy. He went on to play for Southampton, Crystal Palace and Wolverhampton Wanderers before signing for Plymouth in 1968. He made 105 League appearances for Argyle, leaving the club for Bristol City in 1971.

LIONS MAULED

The day that Plymouth Argyle brought to an end Millwall's fine unbeaten home record, stretching back some 59 matches, in January 1967 has been well documented, if only for the 'wrong' reasons. Argyle won 2-1, and amazingly just to show what an upset the result really was, it was their first away win of the season! Unfortunately some of Millwall's supporters could not face defeat, and decided to seek revenge on the team that dared eclipse the Lions at The Den. There followed some quite disgusting scenes of unprovoked violence.

As the Argyle team walked off the pitch they were kicked, jostled and spat upon by Millwall fans who had run on to the playing area amid quite frightening scenes. Even the Plymouth directors did not escape the wrath of the home supporters, as Argyle's Harry Deans was attacked in the directors box!

The Plymouth party of players and officials had travelled to London by train, and then proceeded from there to the Millwall ground by coach. As they boarded the coach for the return journey, windows were smashed by various objects being hurled at it by Millwall yobs who had congregated outside the ground to wait for the Plymouth team. A brick smashed the windscreen showering glass all over the interior of the vehicle. It was quite remarkable, and very lucky, that no-one was badly injured.

So what of the game? Well, for John Mitten, signed on the morning of the match from Coventry City, it was to be a debut he would certainly remember. Alan Banks and Mike Bickle were the Argyle goalscoring heroes which dented the Lions proud home record. The Plymouth team lined up as follows:

Peter Shearing, John Sillett, Doug Baird, Norman Piper, John Newman, Johnny Hore, Barrie Jones, Alan Banks, Mike Bickle, Jimmy Bloomfield, John Mitten. The Argyle substitute was Duncan Neale.

LOTTERY

Plymouth Argyle led the footballing world! In 1977 Argyle became pioneers in organising a club lottery, which was to prove so successful that a number of other clubs quickly copied this profit-making fundraising idea. So successful was the scheme that 'The Argyle Lottery', along with promoter Bill Pearce who introduced the idea, was the subject of much media attention in newspapers and it even received national television coverage. Several clubs were to visit Home Park and talk to Bill Pearce about this fundraising winner, including Celtic, Everton, Leicester City, Newcastle United, West Bromwich Albion and Wolverhampton Wanderers.

The Lottery raised many thousands of pounds for the Argyle cause and has been copied throughout the country by Football League and non-league clubs.

The first draw of the Argyle Lottery took place on 28th September 1977. It was reported that the following thirteen lotteries grossed a total of £130,000 with £45,000 paid in prize money, and over £58,000 profit for Plymouth Argyle. As well as cash prizes several star prizes were on offer such as furniture, jewellery, music centres etc.

MANAGERS

Argyle Manager Robert Jack had three sons who played at Bolton, namely David, Donald and Robert Rollo. Robert Jack managed Argyle during the 1905/06 season, before taking a similar position at Southend United. He returned to Plymouth Argyle in 1910, again as manager, a role he combined with the position of club secretary. He retired in 1938, and died five years later in Southend. His ashes were scattered at the war devastated Home Park ground.

David Jack, who later became the first player to score a goal in a Wembley F.A. Cup Final, in 1923, left Plymouth Argyle because it was reported that he could not cope with the barracking of the crowd at Home Park. He was sold to Bolton Wanderers for £3,000 in 1920, and soon proved what a talent he possessed, going on to play for Arsenal and England.

Brotherly magic? When Plymouth were enjoying promotion from Division Three in 1958/59 they were managed by Jack Rowley. His brother, Arthur, was manager of Shrewsbury Town who won promotion the same season from Division Four!

Vic Buckingham, who was manager of Plymouth Argyle in 1963, albeit

This picture of the Argyle 1957/58 team shows Manager Jack Rowley sat amongst his players. Back row (L to R) G. Adams, B. Jasper, I. L. Griffiths, G. R. T. Barnsley, R. G. Wyatt, H. T. Brown, J. T. Nightingale, M. Kimberley, P. J. Langman. Middle row (L to R) G. Taylor (Trainer), R. Shorthouse, G. Peach, P. Jones, D. Jones, G. Robertson, J. Williams, I. Lavers, H. R. Tilley, H. Penk, G. Reed (Trainer). Front row (L to R) P. Anderson, W. Carter, T. Baker, C. Dougall, J. F. Rowley (Manager), H. N. Langman, K. S. Mitchell, G. P. Quinn, C. Twissell.

for a short period of time, almost became the Argyle boss three years earlier, but declined the offer to take charge of Sheffield Wednesday instead. Buckingham could be the subject of an interesting quiz question, for he was in charge of Argyle for only six weeks in the close season of 1963, and therefore never saw his team play in a competitive match!

In February 1968 Plymouth Argyle were reported to be paying newly appointed manager Billy Bingham £5,000 per annum, the highest wage they had offered any previous manager in their history. In addition Bingham was given an incentive of receiving £2,000 if he could keep Argyle in the Second Division. Unfortunately he did not collect the bonus, for Plymouth finished bottom of the Second Division and were duly relegated.

Bingham had actually been appointed on the recommendation of Torquay United manager Frank O'Farrell, who had been Argyle's first choice for the Home Park 'hot seat'. O'Farrell turned the Plymouth job down, but then suggested Bingham for the post.

The much travelled and charismatic manager John Bond was offered the position of club coach by Plymouth Argyle in May 1970, but just as he was about to accept, A.F.C. Bournemouth asked Bond to be their manager. Bond agreed and declined Argyle's offer.

Lennie Lawrence was caretaker manager of Plymouth Argyle in 1978 for just five games, until the appointment of Malcolm Allison to the post.

Charismatic Malcolm Allison signs autographs for Argyle supporters.

Lawrence later managed Charlton Athletic and Middlesbrough.

How many times have we all heard managers receiving a vote of confidence, only to be dispensed with shortly after? Argyle Chairman Stuart Dawe's match programme notes in April 1983 stated: "The atmosphere behind the scenes at Plymouth Argyle is really first class. The relationship between the board and all the staff is excellent and a lot of credit must go to the Management for the role they are playing to foster this strong family spirit between all departments." Changes in football take place at an alarming rate, and just five months later that strong family spirit was broken when manager Bobby Moncur was to part company with the club by mutual consent.

Between 1903 and 1992 there have been 22 different incumbents of the Manager's position at Plymouth Argyle. They are Frank Brettell (1903/05), Robert Jack (1905/06), William Fullerton (1906/07), Robert Jack (again – 1910/1938), Jack Tresadern (1938/48), Jimmy Rae (1948/55), Jack Rowley (1955/60), Neil Dougall (1960/61), Ellis Stuttard (1961/1963), Vic Buckingham (1963), Andy Beattie (1963/64), Malcolm Allison (1964/65), Derek Ufton (1965/68), Billy Bingham (1968/70), Ellis Stuttard (again – 1970/72), Tony Waiters (1972/77), Mike Kelly (1977/78), Lennie Lawrence (1978), Malcolm Allison (again – 1978/79)), Bobby Saxton 1979/81), Bobby Moncur (1981/83), John Hore (1983/84), Dave Smith (1984/88), Ken Brown (1988/90), David Kemp (1990/92) and Peter Shilton (1992 – to date).

Ellis Stuttard and Bobby Saxton have managed both Plymouth Argyle and their Devon neighbours, Exeter City. John Hore also had a spell as caretaker manager at Exeter.

The first ever manager of Plymouth Argyle in 1903 was Frank Brettell. He had previously been Secretary at Bolton Wanderers and Manager at Tottenham Hotspur and Portsmouth. Brettell was persuaded to leave Portsmouth for Plymouth by Captain F. Windrum, who was formerly a director at the south coast club, and attended the inaugural meeting forming a professional club in Plymouth. Brettell was Argyle's manager for two years until joining the club's board of directors.

MASCOTS AND LUCKY CHARMS

The captain of the Plymouth Argyle team was presented with a lucky charm with a difference before the final league match of the 1929/30 season. The 23,459 spectators were in celebratory mood long before the kick-off for the Division Three South fixture at Home Park against Watford, for Argyle were to win promotion in style as League Champions by defeating their visitors 2-1. Before the game, however, Argyle's Freddie Titmuss was given an enormous pasty by a group of supporters as a good luck charm. It was so big that it was placed on a stretcher (was it ill?) behind one of the goals!

The idea of a lucky pasty cropped up again several times. On one such occasion another huge pasty was paraded through the streets of London, much to the amusement and curiosity of all those who saw it! The pasty was adorned in appropriate coloured ribbons before Argyle's fourth round F.A. Cup tie at Chelsea in January 1936. Unfortunately it did not prove to be so lucky as the one for the aforementioned Watford game, for Plymouth crashed to a 4-1 defeat.

A lucky black cat, stuffed variety, was given to Plymouth Argyle's captain, Moses Russell, prior to the kick-off at Home Park for the third round F.A. Cup tie, again against Chelsea in February 1921. The lucky cat, along with over twenty seven thousand spectators, saw Argyle draw 0-0. The replay also ended goalless, but the second replay back at Home Park saw Chelsea edge through to the next round by 2-1. One wonders what happened to the stuffed cat following that result?

MATCHES

Aberdare Athletic have visited Home Park on six occasions for Third Division South fixtures. The games were played between 1921 and 1927, and the Welshmen lost the lot! They must have hated travelling to Plymouth Argyle, for they lost 0-3, 0-2, 0-2, 0-2, 2-7 and 0-2 in successive visits!

Home Park staged the only competitive match to be played in the country on 3rd February 1940. A meagre crowd of 896, with probably more serious matters on their minds than just football, witnessed a goal feast as Plymouth Argyle romped to a 10-3 win against Bristol City in a wartime South West Regional League fixture. Four of the Argyle goals were scored by Brentford player Len Townsend who was stationed locally, whilst the Bristol City team contained two guest players from Torquay United.

The size of crowds varied enormously during the 1939/40 season, with football low down on most people's priorities. Whilst the 896 present for the Bristol City game was the lowest of that particular season, only two months earlier over four thousand had watched Argyle entertain Newport County, Plymouth winning 2-0.

The last trip Plymouth Argyle made to the ill-fated Accrington Stanley Football Club was for the penultimate match of the 1958/59 season. Stanley were to resign from the Football League in October 1962 due to their financial problems. Argyle travelled to Peel Park on 25th April 1959 in good heart, for they were to finish the season as Division Three Champions. An attendance of four thousand were present to witness pint-sized Argyle winger Harry Penk score for the Pilgrims in a 1-1 draw.

Plymouth Argyle and Huddersfield Town must have been sick of the sight of each other in the 1963/64 season, for they played each other no fewer than six times! Not only did they meet in the League, but they were also drawn against each other in both the Football League Cup and the F.A. Cup. Argyle didn't manage to win one game! In the Second Division they lost 4-3 at Huddersfield, and drew 0-0 at Home Park. The League Cup meeting went to three matches. A 2-2 draw at Home Park was followed by a 3-3 draw in the replay at Huddersfield. A second replay took place on the neutral ground of Aston Villa with Huddersfield winning 2-1. In the third round of the F.A. Cup Huddersfield again travelled to Plymouth, and won 1-0.

Plymouth Argyle met Middlesborough three times in the space of eight days in the 1990/91 season. Plymouth had to make the long journey to Ayresome Park on Saturday, 5th January 1991 for a third round F.A. Cup tie. They drew 0-0 before 13,042 spectators. It was back on the long trek to Middlesbrough a week later for a Second Division fixture and another goalless scoreline, this time watched by a crowd of 14,198. Forty eight hours later it was Middlesbrough's turn to travel to Home Park for the F.A. Cup replay. At last goals were scored, but unfortunately for Argyle they managed only one, a penalty netted by Nicky Marker, whilst Middlesbrough scored twice through Ian Baird and Paul Kerr, to disappoint many of the 6,956 strong crowd.

It is not often that Plymouth Argyle have entertained Scottish League opposition. Aberdeen visited Home Park in May 1951 for a testimonial match for defender Bill Strauss, and two weeks later Ayr United were the visitors for a match as part of the Festival of Britain celebrations. Three days later Argyle played another Festival of Britain match, but at the more modest surroundings of Chippenham Town's ground.

Another Scottish club to play at Home Park were the now famous defunct Glasgow-based club of Third Lanark, who provided friendly opposition for Plymouth in April 1953.

Although Plymouth Argyle entered the Anglo-Scottish Cup in 1977/78, they never met a Scottish League club! The early stages were played on a group basis, with the winners going forward to the Quarter Finals to meet Scottish opponents. Argyle never made it, finishing third in their four team group consisting of Birmingham City, Bristol City and Bristol Rovers.

OVERSEAS PLAYERS

Plymouth Argyle have had a number of overseas-born players on their books who include Doug Anderson (Hong Kong), David Phillips (West Germany), Bill Strauss (South Africa), Erik Van Rossum (Holland) and Stan Williams (South Africa).

Inside forward Crawford Clelland was born in New Jersey, in the U.S.A., although as his name obviously suggests he had strong links with Scotland.

Th Argyle team of 1971/72 includes Peta Balac who left Argyle to go to South Africa. Back row (L to R) Ronald Brown, Pat Allen, Dave Burnside, John Hore, Don Hutchins, Paul Chapman, Allan Harris, Derek Rickard, Les Latcham. Third row (L to R) Tony Ford, Stephen Davey, Colin Norman, Jimmy Hinch, Keith Allen, Jim Furnell, Dave Provan, Mike Bickle, Mike Dowling, Colin Sullivan, Bill Shearer. Second row (L to R) Bryan Edwards, C. W. Crookes, S. J. Williams, P. W. Skinnard, Bobby Saxton, E. Stuttard, B. S. Williams, T. H. Deans, G. A. Little. Front row (L to R) John Dent, Keith Sullivan, Arthur Blamey, Jimmy Jennings, Alan Holloway, Alan Rogers, Peter Darke, Peta Balac.

Argyle actually signed the player from Aberdeen in 1955.

Two Polish Navy players stationed at Devonport were signed on amateur forms by Plymouth Argyle in November 1946. Both inside forwards, they were Herbert Gruszka, aged 25, and Francis Pelczyk, 23. Neither made the first team.

A few players have left Plymouth Argyle to try their luck 'overseas'. They include: Doug Anderson (Hong Kong 1989), Peta Balac (South Africa 1973), Tony Brimacombe (South Africa 1968), John Clayton (Germany 1988), John Craven (Canada 1978), Keith Furphy (U.S.A. 1987), David Kemp (U.S.A. 1982) and Mike Reeves (South Africa 1970).

OWN GOAL

Every football supporter can probably remember seeing an own goal, some of which are pure classics. Every team registers a dreaded 'o.g.' at some stage, although perhaps not as much in present day football, for players now claim goals that are going hopelessly wide until being deflected past the goalkeeper into the net.

Leicester City players managed to score two own goals in the Second Division match at Home Park in February 1947. The unfortunate players who helped Plymouth to a 4-0 win were David Jones and Seph Smith.

Bournemouth and Boscombe Athletic repeated the feat of scoring twice in their own net when they came to Plymouth in November 1957. Harry Hughes and Alan Rule were on the scoresheet, as was Argyle's Jimmy Gauld, Plymouth winning 3-1.

Shrewsbury Town pair John Moore and Alf Wood managed to score an own goal each in the 4-4 draw at Plymouth in November 1970.

One own goal involving Plymouth Argyle, described as 'The Weirdest Goal Ever' by the *Western Gazette* newspaper, involved the Second Division match at Home Park against Fulham in October 1954. The Londoners' goalkeeper Frank Elliott badly hurt his wrist in a challenge for the ball with Argyle centre forward Neil Langman. Although the ball was safely in his grasp, Elliott rolled over in obvious pain and distress, some fifteen yards from his goal. He then threw the ball over his shoulder and into his own net! It was not a happy day for Fulham who went on to lose both their goalkeeper with a broken wrist, and the game 3-2.

The most memorable own goal performance surely belongs to Mansfield Town's Terry Swinscoe, who not content to score once, did it again in the same match at Home Park in March 1959. His brace of own goals certainly did not help matters as far as Mansfield were concerned, crashing to an 8-3 defeat. Swinscoe could not have been very popular with his team mates!

PADDLE STEAMERS

Swansea Town supporters can recall the occasion when a few adventurous North Devon-based Plymouth Argyle fans made the journey to the Vetch Field ground by Paddle Steamer! An excursion from Ilfracombe to Swansea was operated by the locally based Paddle Steamer Company which coincided with Argyle's match at Swansea in Easter 1947. One Argyle follower spent most of the game beating a tune on a big base drum throughout the entire ninety minutes. Sadly, the intrepid seafaring followers returned to Devon having seen Argyle go down 3 goals to 1, Bill Strauss being the Plymouth goalscorer.

PENALTIES

It is something of a risky business for a goalkeeper to be entrusted with the taking of penalty kicks, especially if he misses! However, Argyle keeper Fred Craig scored no less than five times from the spot in Football League fixtures, including three in one season. His successes came in 1926/27 at Home Park against Brentford, Newport County and Charlton Athletic. Plymouth won all three matches, 2-1, 3-1 and 4-1 respectively. Craig netted again in the final match of the following season at Crystal Palace, when Argyle won 2-0. His fifth and final league goal came in 1929/30 when he scored the winning goal from the penalty spot in a thrilling 4-3 victory over rivals Torquay United at Plainmoor.

Tony McShane achieved the rare feat of scoring a hat-trick of penalties in Plymouth Argyle reserves' 3-1 win over Portsmouth, in the Football Combination in August 1952.

Cardiff City missed two penalties in the same match against Plymouth Argyle at Ninian Park in the 1959/60 season. Brian Walsh missed the target altogether with the first spot kick awarded. Then Argyle keeper Geoff Barnsley blocked the second penalty from Dennis Malloy. The misses proved costly for Cardiff as Argyle won 1-0 thanks to a Wilf Carter first-half header.

Argyle goalkeeper Paul Barron had to face an amazing four penalty kicks in the Football League Cup first round tie at Exeter City in August 1977. City's Lammie Robertson scored with two, the first of which was a twice taken kick after another Exeter player had moved into the area. Another penalty kick, the fourth of the game, again taken by Robertson, was saved by Barron. The game ended in a 2-2 draw.

Argyle goalkeeper Neil Hards saved a penalty on his Football

This photograph of the Argyle team of 1958/59 includes goalkeeper Geoff Barnsley. Back row (L to R) G. R. Fincham, G. T. Barrett, G. R. Barnsley, R. G. Wyllie, E. Doughty, R. G. Wyatt. Middle row (L to R) G. Taylor (Trainer), G. W. Adams, J. L. Williams, G. Robertson, C. Dougall, D. Downs, J. Sim, D. J. Hancock, G. Reed (Asst Trainer). Front row (L to R) P. D. Anderson, C. Twissell, J. Gauld, C. W. Crookes (Director), R. J. R. Blindell (Chairman), W. Carter, T. G. Baker, H. Penk.

League debut for the club against Bury at Home Park on the opening day of the 1979/80 season. His save helped Plymouth to a 2-0 win.

PERSIL

Football clubs are forever looking at ways at cutting costs and Plymouth Argyle were no different in the 1979/80 season, although it was a cost-cutting exercise which brought with it a good deal of publicity. The well-known washing powder brand, Persil, had a rail travel promotion scheme whereby packet tops were collected to enable two persons to travel for the price of one. Argyle quickly decided to utilise the scheme, travelling by train to their games at Brentford and Reading among others. Not only did this save money (the kit lady had plenty of Persil!) but also it was explained that the players appreciated a change at not having to travel by coach as was the usual practice. Secretary Graham Little, in his programme notes for one particular match, thanked supporters who had handed in Persil coupons to his office, especially the anonymous person who posted some from Exeter!

PLAYERS

Up until the commencement of the 1992/93 season, it is believed that Plymouth Argyle have never signed a first team player from Halifax Town, Hartlepool, Huddersfield Town, Lincoln City, Peterborough United, Rochdale, Shrewsbury Town, Wigan Athletic or Wrexham.

Up until the commencement of the 1992/93 season it is believed that Plymouth Argyle have never transferred a player to Barnet, Darlington, Doncaster Rovers, Leicester City or Sheffield Wednesday.

When Plymouth Argyle entered the Southern League in 1903, they went for experienced players in their side to guide the club through the first few seasons. It was so 'experienced' that other clubs cruelly dubbed the Argyle side as being the 'scrap iron team'! England cricketer C.B. Fry had another name for the newly formed Plymouth team – 'The Dandies' – on account of Argyle's smart playing strip of green and black!

Tragedy struck the club in that first season when Wattie Anderson, who had been signed from Woolwich Arsenal, died of pneumonia. He had played in Plymouth Argyle's Southern League fixture at Fulham in February 1904, but Watson was admitted to hospital soon after, and sadly lost his fight for life.

The first professional playing staff at Home Park in 1903 consisted of Robert Jack (from Glossop), Johnny Banks (from Manchester United), Andrew Clark (East Fife), Charlie Clark (Everton), Bob Dalrymple (Hearts), Harry Digweed (Portsmouth), Jack Fitchett (Bolton Wanderers), Archie Goodall (Derby County), Charlie Hare (Aston Villa), Billy Leech (Stoke City), Jack Peddie (Manchester United), Jack Picken (Bolton Wanderers), Jack Robinson (Southampton), Harry Winterhalder (Wednesday) plus the aforementioned Wattie Anderson from Woolwich Arsenal.

Half back Billy Baker, one of Plymouth Argyle's stalwarts in the early days of the club's existence, was killed in action in France during the First World War. Baker had been signed from Plymouth club Green Waves in 1909, and went on to make 197 appearances before being called upon to join the Army six years later.

Jack Wharton scored on his debut for Plymouth Argyle in the Second Division fixture against West Bromwich Albion in November 1938. Almost exactly twenty three years later his son, Terry, was to score on his debut for Wolverhampton Wanderers against Ipswich Town.

Several Argyle players have combined the sports of football and cricket. These include William Baker who appeared for Plymouth between 1921 and 1927, as well as playing cricket for the local Plymouth club and for Devon.

Jack Chisholm had been on the staff at Middlesex County Cricket Club, and took many wickets with his fast bowling in Minor Counties cricket for Bedfordshire. Chisholm made 187 League and Cup appearances for Plymouth Argyle between 1949 and 1955.

George Dews (Worcestershire), nicknamed 'Gentleman George', and Barry Meyer, the latter later becoming a County Cricket umpire, were another two who successfully combined both sports.

Bill Strauss who played for Argyle between 1946 and 1954, made a number of appearances for Devon County Cricket Club, as did inside

This picture of the 1947/48 Argyle team includes Bill Strauss, Ernie Carless, Bill Shortt and Len Boyd. They line up as follows: Back Row (L to R) J. Oakes, S. Dixon, R. Pengelly, M. Tadman, S. Rawlings, B. Purvis, R. Warren, W. Adams, C. Miller, A. Knight. Third row (L to R) B. Greenaway, A. Holland, J. Davies, G. Silk, G. Wright, W. Shortt, D. Thomas, S. Rundle, C. Livsey, L. Boyd. Second row (L to R) R. Gorman, P. Ratcliffe, W. Strauss, P. Jones, L. Jones, Mr Tresadern, Mr J. Rae, E. Stuttard, J. Buist, A. Miller, R. Royston, W. Harper. Front row (L to R) E. Carless, R. Tregaskis, A. Hall, L. Tinkler, M. Murphy, F. Mitcheson, J. Mulholland.

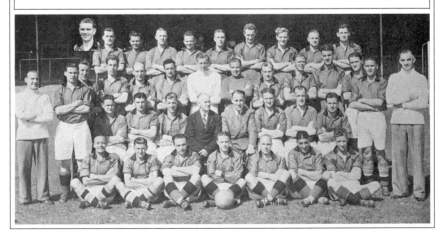

forward Ernie Carless who was at Home Park in the 1946/47 season.

Pat Glover and goalkeeper Bill Shortt both played for Wales in unofficial International matches during the Second World War. Glover lined up for Wales against England at Ninian Park, Cardiff in November 1939, and scored the only Welsh goal in the 1-1 draw. Shortt also won Welsh honours, but against Northern Ireland in May 1946. The match was also played at Ninian Park and ended in a single goal victory for the Irish.

Len Boyd was signed by Plymouth Argyle in somewhat unusual circumstances. Boyd serving with the Royal Navy in Malta in 1945, was recommended to the club by an Argyle supporter who was a colleague. He wrote to Argyle for signing on forms, which the club duly dispatched! Boyd, an inside forward, was obviously a good signing, for after 78 League appearances for Plymouth he commanded a £17,500 transfer fee on his move to Birmingham City in January 1949.

Big 'Jumbo' Jack Chisholm was the man to settle disputes on behalf of his fellow players whilst at Plymouth Argyle. No-one argued and won with Jumbo! In January 1950 the Argyle board of directors refused to pay the players a bonus should they achieve a result against the then F.A. Cup holders, Wolverhampton Wanderers, at Home Park in the third round. After Chisholm's strong protestations, the board agreed to pay up.

Former Everton goalkeeper Ted Sager holds the record for the longest career with a single Football League club – 24 years and 1 month. He ended his Everton career in a match at Home Park in November 1952. Plymouth Argyle won the match, but Sager only conceded one goal, that being scored by Neil Dougall.

The Swiggs family have represented Plymouth Argyle in League matches on two separate occasions. Centre forward Robert Swiggs made two appearances in the 1955/56 season, and had one further outing the following season. His son, Bradley, a prolific goalscorer at non-league level, made his Argyle league debut in May 1984 at Gillingham. He made one further substitute appearance before being released. Bradley was playing his football for Jewson South Western League side, Launceston in 1992/93.

Another father and son combination at Argyle is that of Steve and Joe Davey. Steve made over two hundred League appearances for Plymouth between 1967 and 1975, before moving on to Portsmouth, Hereford United and Exeter City. His son, Joe, was signed as a Y.T.S. player for Queens Park Rangers, but he could not settle in the London area, and joined Argyle at the start of the 1992/93 season to try and make the grade as a full professional.

Argyle winger Charlie Twissell appeared for the Great Britain team at the 1956 Melbourne Olympic Games. He had made his debut for Plymouth as an amateur a year earlier after leaving the Royal Navy, and went on to win six England Amateur International caps, before eventually turning professional at Home Park.

Taunton Town protested to the Football Association with regards to the alleged illegal means by which forward Stuart Brace was signed by Plymouth Argyle. Taunton asked the Football Association in December 1960 for their observations on the transfer. The result was that the F.A. were to take no action over the matter. Argyle had offered to send the first team to Taunton at the end of the season for a friendly match which would have raised funds for the Somerset club, but Plymouth chairman Ron Blindell said their offer had been ignored. Brace only made nine League appearances for Plymouth, but enjoyed much more success after leaving Home Park when he played for Watford, Mansfield Town, Peterborough United, Grimsby Town and Southend United.

Inside forward Alan O'Neil, who joined Plymouth Argyle in 1962 from Aston Villa, was actually born with the name Alan Hope. He changed his name to O'Neil on signing in 1955 for his first League Club Sunderland. O'Neil was transferred from Argyle to Bournemouth in 1963.

Tony Book

Tony Book was signed by Argyle manager Malcolm Allison from Bath City in 1964 for £1,500 at the age of 29. Until then Book had played all his football at non-league level and worked as a bricklayer. Allison has been quoted as saying that a Bath City director was laughing when he offered £1,500 for Book, but it was Plymouth Argyle and Tony Book who were to have the last laugh! Sold for £17,000 to Manchester City in July 1966, Book made 242 appearances for the Maine Road club, and later had a spell as Manager and was still on the coaching staff there in 1991/92.

The oldest player to make his Football League debut for Plymouth Argyle is Player-Manager and goalkeeper Peter Shilton, who at the age of 42 years and 199 days lined up for Argyle in a goalless draw away to Charlton Athletic on 4th April 1992. This was a game that took place at West Ham United's Upton Park ground, the Charlton club temporarily sharing the facilities for the 1991/92 season.

John Oakes, another 42-year-old, who was signed on a free transfer from Charlton Athletic, made his League debut against Newcastle United in

August 1947 which ended in a 6-1 defeat for Argyle. Oakes made 36 League appearances for Plymouth, captaining the side, but was released at the end of the 1947/48 season and joined Kent non-league side Snowdon Colliery.

The fastest goalscoring milkman in the West was striker Mike Bickle. He worked as a milkman for Co-operative Society, and played for their team in the Devon Wednesday League, as well as South Western League St Austell at the weekend. Bickle's goalscoring prowess soon took preference over the delivering of 'gold tops' and he signed as a professional for Plymouth Argyle in December 1965. Bickle went on to score 71 League goals for the Pilgrims, and ended his career at Gillingham where he spent one season.

Another goalscoring milkman to play for Plymouth Argyle was Ian Pearson, although he did not actually start his dairy business until leaving

There are many familiar faces in this Argle team. Ian Pearson is in the front row fourth from the left.

the club for Exeter City. Pearson had been signed in 1974 from non-league Goole Town and later appeared for Millwall and Exeter. Pearson returned to Home Park for a second spell with Argyle in 1983.

Plymouth Argyle defender John Hore, who went on to play in four hundred Football League matches for the club, before spending another five seasons at Exeter City, was signed as an apprentice at Home Park after travelling back from a trial match with Stoke City. Argyle scout Ellis Stuttard contacted Hore's parents whilst John was away at Stoke, but he had no hesitation in travelling back to Devon and signing for Plymouth.

Two Plymouth Argyle players hit the newspaper headlines for all the wrong reasons in September 1968. During the course of the Third Division match at Stockport County feelings began to run high, particularly as far as defender Fred Molyneux and striker Mike Bickle were concerned. The two were seen to exchange angry words, and actually square up to each other. Argyle eventually won the game 3-2, with Bickle scoring one of the goals. Needless to say both players were severely censured by Argyle boss Billy Bingham.

Ipswich Town paid their then record transfer fee of £220,000 for Plymouth Argyle striker Paul Mariner in October 1976. The fee included two players, Terry Austin and John Peddelty, moving from Ipswich to Plymouth as part of the deal. Mariner had been signed by Argyle from Chorley in 1973, and scored 56 league goals during his stay at Home Park.

The record for the quickest booking seen at Home Park belongs to Micky Horswill who managed to get his name in the referee's notebook after just seven seconds. Horswill was making his first appearance back at Plymouth after being transferred from Argyle to Hull City. The game, played in April 1979, ended in a 4-3 win for the Pilgrims.

Plymouth Argyle started a Football Centre of Excellence in September 1984 to encourage and develop promising youngsters on the road to a possible career in the game. This proved very successful. The idea of grooming possible future stars was first mooted by director Mr Burroughs, manager John Hore, and Dave Babb, who was to become the director of the Centre of Excellence.

Versatile defender Nick Marker has found himself keeping goal for Plymouth Argyle on at least three occasions during the course of first team fixtures. In the 1990/91 season he took over between the posts in a Rumbelows Cup (Football League Cup) match at Wimbledon when regular keeper Rhys Wilmott was sent off. The following season he again deputised for Wilmott, who was injured during the league fixture at Newcastle United. In August 1992, Marker replaced Player-manager Peter Shilton, who had been sent off in the game at Hull City, and promptly saved a penalty taken by Leigh Jenkinson, and also the follow-up effort from Gary Lund.

Marker figured in a transfer deal reported to be worth £500,000 when he left Home Park for Blackburn Rovers in September 1992. Marker was valued at £250,000, whilst two players of similar combined value left Blackburn for Plymouth as part of the deal. Winger Craig Skinner (already on loan at Argyle) and defender Keith Hill were the players involved.

Long serving midfielder Kevin Hodges broke the Plymouth Argyle appearance record on August 25th 1990 in the game at Newcastle United. It was appearance number 471 for Hodges, who began his career at Argyle in 1976 as an apprentice professional. By the end of the 1991/92 season, Hodges was on his way to making his 550th appearance for the club. The previous record holder was Sammy Black.

Argyle twice broke their transfer fee record for buying players during the

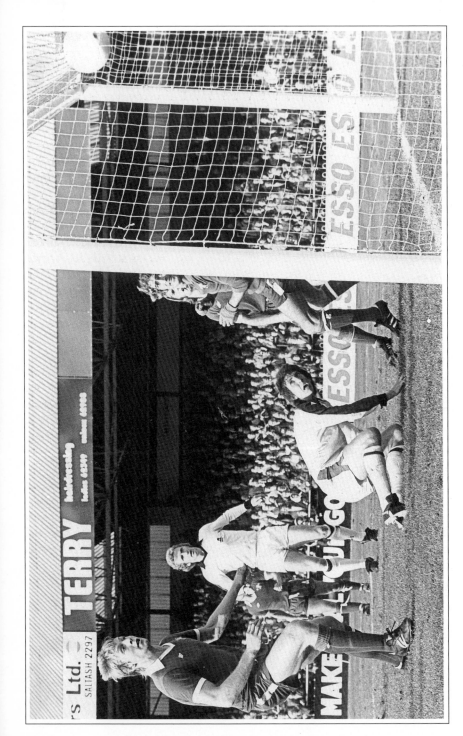

1991/92 season. Newly appointed millionaire club chairman Dan McCauley and his board of directors authorised manager Dave Kemp to pay £200,000 to Notts County for striker Dave Regis. A few months later Kemp had been sacked, but his replacement, Player-Manager Peter Shilton then splashed out £250,000 for another striker, this time Kevin Nugent from Leyton Orient. Regis had an unhappy first few months at Home Park and was transfer listed in May 1992 but after a spell on loan with A.F.C. Bournemouth he regained a first team place at Argyle again.

The spending spree continued at the start of the following season, when the club transfer record was reported to have been equalled once more with the arrival of winger Paul Dalton from Hartlepool. The move involved Argyle player Ryan Cross moving to Hartlepool. It was stated that Argyle paid £200,000 for Dalton, but they also valued Cross at £50,000 – thus the deal involved £250,000. Dalton, like Regis, had an unhappy start to his Argyle career, sustaining an injury in a pre-season match which sidelined the player for a number of weeks.

Until the 1991/92 season, the record fee that Argyle had paid was £170,000 for Mark Smith from Sheffield Wednesday in 1987.

Home sweet home? At least eight players who have appeared in Football League matches for the club have left Plymouth Argyle, only to return to Home Park for a second spell. They are: Jeff Cook (1979 and 1981/1983), Arthur Davies (1935/1937, 1938/39), Ernie Edds (1946/1949, 1953/1955), Alex Govan (1946/1953, 1958/1960), Frank Lord (1963/1966, 1967/1968), Ian Pearson (1974/1977 and 1983) and Colin Randell (1973/1977, 1979/1982).

Prolific goalscorer Tommy Tynan has actually had three spells at Argyle! He originally joined the club in 1983 from Newport County, leaving for Rotherham United in 1985. He then returned to Home Park on loan from Rotherham before going back to the Yorkshire team. Tynan was then signed by Argyle in 1986, staying at Plymouth until his transfer to Torquay United in 1990.

PROFESSIONALISM

The step of forming a professional football club in Plymouth became reality following an enthusiastic meeting held at Chubb's Hotel in East Street. Many of those present at the meeting had been connected with the football section of the Argyle Athletic Club. It was decided that the people of Plymouth were ready to support a professional club, after a great deal of success at amateur level.

A limited company was formed, and directors elected. Home Park was to be the headquarters of the new Plymouth Argyle club, and it was decided to seek election to the Southern League. Frank Brettell was appointed team manager, having previously been in charge at Portsmouth.

After much lobbying among Southern League clubs, Plymouth Argyle were eventually accepted into the competition, but not before they had agreed to defray the travelling expenses of all visiting clubs to Home Park during their first season of membership to the league.

PROGRAMMES

There was a time when virtually every spectator bought a match programme, if only to find the respective team line-ups. We are now in the age of magazines rather than programmes, or as one collector so aptly described them – "All gloss and dross." Plymouth Argyle programmes have also moved with the times, gone are the days of basic but informative programmes, now it is a case of professionally written and printed versions with a splash of colour to liven up the 'proceedings'.

Those programmes from the 1940s and '50s somehow evoke a sense of nostalgia. Where else would you find for instance an article in a Plymouth Argyle programme for a match in the 1955/56 season entitled – "Slow Handclap. The Scourge of Soccer." Argyle today would no doubt be quite happy if they only had a slow hand clap to contend with – no more trouble with visiting supporters and only a mere handful of police needed at matches!

A survey was undertaken by a national magazine – *Programme Monthly* – in 1983 to find the oldest Plymouth Argyle programme still known to be in existence. This proved to be an issue for a Southern League fixture at Home Park against Reading in September 1906. It was thought however that programmes could have been on sale during the 1903/04 season, although this was not confirmed by anyone participating in the survey.

The match programme issued during the 1937/38 season consisted of 28 pages, heavily laden with advertisements, but cost the princely sum of two old pennies. Two prominent advertisements appeared on the front cover, along with the relevant match details. They were for Genoni's Swiss Restaurant, situated opposite the old Theatre Royal, for a 'Perfect Lunch or Dinner', and if the weather was a little inclement, then Wakeling's Umbrellas in George Street, Plymouth, could be the answer. They described their brollies as 'strong, durable and cheap', and what's more they had 'an enormous stock to choose from'. Another advertisement to catch the eye was for the purchase of a brand new Morris saloon car for the bargain price of £209.

Inevitably the cost of buying a Plymouth Argyle programme has risen

---

Fleet-footed Tommy Tynan in action for Argyle.

over the years. In 1963 for instance, reading about your favourite team would cost four old pennies (less than 2p converted into today's currency)! Ten years later the price had risen to 5p, and by 1983 it had jumped to 35p. The price continued to climb sharply, the programme for the 1991/92 season costing £1.

PROMOTION

Plymouth Argyle have achieved the 'goal' of promotion in the Football League on five occasions, each time winning a place in Division Two. They won the Third Division South Championship in 1929/30 and 1951/52, the Third Division Championship in 1958/59, and have twice been Third Division runners-up in 1974/75 and 1985/86.

The first occasion that Argyle achieved promotion in 1929/30 was particularly noteworthy in that they remained unbeaten from the opening day 2-0 win at Clapton Orient, until they lost 1-0 at Coventry City on Christmas Day. The unbeaten run stretched over eighteen League matches, twelve of which were won. A quite remarkable record.

Needless to say there were ecstatic scenes of sheer joy for Argyle's last game of the season. 23,459 spectators acclaimed their heroes for the final

Jumbo Chisholm leads the promotion-winning Argyle team of 1952 out on to the pitch to play Torquay United.

fixture against Watford. Argyle did not let their faithful supporters down, as they ended the season in style with a 2-1 win. Three weeks later the team made a tour of the city of Plymouth, and thousands thronged the streets to celebrate Argyle's success.

It was perhaps fitting that on the second occasion that Argyle achieved promotion in 1952, the last home fixture was against neighbouring Torquay United. This allowed for a bumper attendance at Home Park of 28,728. Before the kick off, the Torquay team applauded the Argyle players on to the field led by 'Jumbo' Chisholm holding aloft a green and white umbrella.

Three Plymouth Argyle players who were members of the first team during promotion winning seasons, have also appeared in similar promotion winning sides for Exeter City after leaving Home Park. They are – John Hore, Bobby Saxton and Darren Rowbotham.

'Q' CLUBS AND PLAYERS

The first player to make the move from Queens Park Rangers to Plymouth Argyle was co-incidentally an inside forward whose surname began with the letter 'Q'. The player concerned was Gordon Quinn who signed for Argyle in 1956. He only made eleven league appearances for Plymouth, however, scoring two goals, before being released.

The very first player to play for Plymouth Argyle from a 'Q' club was goalkeeper Robert Brown, who played at Home Park during the 1945/46 season. He was stationed in Plymouth, many hundreds of miles from his home club Queens Park, and made just three 'guest' appearances against Southampton, Derby County and Coventry City.

RABBITS

With Home Park being situated in what was a rural setting in their early years, it was not unusual to see wild life encroaching on the playing surface from time to time. The pitch was often frequented by rabbits, and there are several stories relating to matches being stopped whilst they have been chased off the ground! On one occasion in the 1930s it was reported that a training match was halted whilst a rabbit beat a hasty dash from one end of the pitch to the other.

RAIL TRAVEL

The Argyle team faced a difficult overnight train journey to fulfil their Second Division fixture at Everton on 27th December 1930. After playing a Boxing Day afternoon fixture at Home Park against Cardiff City and recording a 5-1 victory, the Plymouth team boarded the train at 8 p.m. arriving on Merseyside ten hours later. Was it really surprising therefore that this horrendous match preparation, which included a few hours sleep at a hotel, ended in a very humiliating 9-1 defeat against Everton who were to become Second Division champions.

Plymouth Argyle supporters frequently took advantage of special excursion rail fares to away fixtures, although the journey times were somewhat protracted in comparison to what one expects today. For example, in December 1960, for just forty four shillings (£2.20), you could go all the way to Ipswich to cheer on the Argyle, however it meant leaving Plymouth on Friday evening at 11.35 p.m. The fare did not include the cost of the Underground between London stations.

REFEREES

An interesting experiment took place at Home Park on 4th May 1953 when Plymouth Argyle played Portsmouth in their Golden Jubilee match. Two referees officiated, one in each half of the pitch. The two 'men in black' were Mr D. L. Scoble from Plymouth, and well-known international referee Mr Jack Wiltshire, who originally hailed from Torpoint. The experiment was obviously not a success, although the idea of two match referees has been mooted on several occasions since.

Heard about the match referee who scored the only goal of the game? This unfortunate incident occurred

Home Park Plymouth

Kick off 6.30 p.m.

Monday, May 4th, 1953

Golden Jubilee Celebration Match

Plymouth Argyle

versus

Portsmouth

OFFICIAL PROGRAMME **3d.**

Printed by E. J. Rickard, St. Judes, Plymouth. 'Phone : 6 0 9 5 5
Published by Plymouth Argyle Football Co. Ltd.

in the Third Division fixture between Barrow and Plymouth Argyle in

November 1968. Unfortunate for Plymouth, because it was against them that Mr Ivan Robinson of Manchester scored the winning goal! A 77th minute shot, which was going at least five yards wide of the target, from Barrow's former Exeter City centre forward George McLean, hit the referee's left foot and flew off in another direction into the net over the head of the astonished Argyle goalkeeper Pat Dunne. Mr Robinson apologised to Argyle after the match and said: "I tried to get out of the way. I was amazed to see the ball go into the net."

RELEGATION

Plymouth Argyle have suffered the disappointment of relegation on five occasions, the most recent being in 1991/92. They have dropped from Division Two into the Third on each occasion in 1949/50, 1955/56, 1967/68 and 1985/86. Although Argyle were relegated at the end of the 1991/92 season, because of the re-organisation of the divisions following the formation of a Premier League, the club still found themselves in the newly named Second Division, which in fact consisted of the previous season's Third Division clubs.

RESERVES

Plymouth Argyle reserves were one of the founder member clubs of the Plymouth and District League in 1905. Other teams in that first season of the league were Essa, Exeter City (first team), Green Waves, Millbrook Rangers,

Jimmy Greaves playing in a Reserve game for Tottenham Hotspur at Home Park on 9th December 1961. Here he is being challenged by John Williams.

Tavistock and Torpoint.

Argyle reserves won the championship of the Plymouth and District League in 1907/08, 1908/09, and 1919/20. They were also runners-up in 1905/06, 1906/07, 1909/10, 1910/11 and 1912/13. Argyle's 'A' team have also been members of the league since those early successes.

After a series of poor performances by the Argyle reserve team in 1961, the board of directors decided drastic action was needed. They placed four players on the transfer list and said: "We must strengthen our reserve side. We are not going to stand for such poor displays, and are certainly not satisfied with the way the reserves have been playing. We are determined to give the supporters better football." The Argyle reserve team were at the time playing in Division Two of the Football Combination, and finally ended the season in a mid-table position of ninth place.

The Argyle reserve team drew a crowd of 12,907 to Home Park in December 1961. If they were honest though they hadn't come along to watch Argyle. They were there to see the return to English football of that ace goalscorer Jimmy Greaves. The England International had signed for Tottenham Hotspur after an unhappy sojourn in Italian League football. His first game was in the Spurs reserves team in this Football Combination fixture at Plymouth. Greaves didn't let his admirers down, for he scored twice in a resounding Spurs 4-1 win.

Argyle withdrew their reserve team from the Football Combination at the end of the 1981/82 season for financial reasons. Lack of numbers, and even fewer professionals with sufficient experience to play at Combination level, eventually persuaded the directors that the team should be pulled out. The following season the Argyle reserve team played their football in the Western League. Attempts have been made to rejoin Combination but existing member clubs are not keen on the long travelling distance involved fulfilling fixtures at Home Park.

The club were back in the Football Combination, however, for the 1992/93 season. A newly formed regionalised division enabled Argyle to enter their reserves once again. The division consisted of Birmingham City, A.F.C Bournemouth, Bristol Rovers, Cardiff City, Cheltenham Town, Exeter City, Swansea City, Torquay United and Yeovil Town.

ROTTERDAM FAN

It's not unusual for football clubs to receive letters from all over the world requesting information, souvenirs, pen friends etc. but in February 1980 Argyle received a letter from a fourteen-year-old lad by the name of Ad Poot, who resided in Rotterdam. He described himself as being an avid Argyle fan having followed their fortunes via the results service of BBC radio and through the columns of the *Sunday People* newspaper. His father said: "My son is crazy! I cannot understand why he should want to support a little Third Division club"!

RUGBY UNION

Goalkeeper J.W. Sutcliffe won international honours for England at both Rugby Union and Association Football. He made 181 first team appearances for Plymouth Argyle between 1904 and 1912. Sutcliffe had been signed by Argyle from Bolton Wanderers, and retired from the game on leaving Home Park.

A couple of important Rugby Union fixtures have been played at Home Park, bringing back memories of the origins of the ground which was originally occupied by the Devonport Albion Rugby Club. In October 1951, the South West Counties side played the touring South African Rugby Union team. Home Park was chosen because of its large capacity, and was so again ten years later when Devon drew 0-0 with Cheshire in the final of the County Championship.

SANTOS SAGA

The stage was set for one of the biggest nights in the club's history when crack Brazilian team Santos visited Home Park for a friendly fixture in March 1973. Undoubtedly the main attraction for the 37,639 crowd which packed into the ground was a unique chance for many to see the silky skills

Several of the players in this team photo lined up to play Santos at Home Park in March 1973.

79

of the world's greatest footballer – Pele.

The game however almost didn't take place, for with supporters still queuing up to enter the Home Park turnstiles, the Santos club officials started to make extra demands instead of the pre-match agreed financial arrangements. They met Argyle chairman Robert Daniel and insisted that the share of gate receipts due to them was paid before kick off. They then tried another tack, by saying they wouldn't play unless Argyle paid them £2,500 more than the agreed sum! The Santos officials were adamant, if they were not paid what they wanted then they would not play the game.

Mr Daniel had by now been placed in a very awkward position. What would happen if the crowd, many of whom had travelled from all corners of the Westcountry, were told that the game had been called off? He did not want to be held to what amounted to 'ransom' by the Brazilians, but rather than have no game at all, Daniel had little choice but to agree to their extra demands.

The game went ahead with the crowd oblivious of what had gone on in those minutes leading up to kick-off. Pele didn't let the large gathering down, displaying his skills, and scoring from the penalty spot in the second half. By then however Argyle had stormed into a 3-0 interval lead with goals from Mike Dowling, Derek Rickard and Jimmy Hinch. Edu pulled a second goal back for Santos to end a memorable evening for more reasons than just the match itself!

The Argyle side that played in the friendly? It lined up as follows: Jim Furnell, Dave Provan, Colin Sullivan, John Hore, Bobby Saxton, Neil Hague, Mike Dowling, Derek Rickard, Jimmy Hinch, Les Latcham and Alan Welsh. Substitutes used were Milija Aleksic for Furnell and Steve Davey for Hinch.

Long serving Argyle defender John Hore still has a proud memento of this special occasion – the very Santos shirt that the great Pele wore in the game.

SENT OFF

No player is proud of being sent off in a game, but no fewer than three Plymouth Argyle players all received their marching orders in the same game on one occasion! What made it even more unusual was that the Third Division match at Port Vale was played on a Sunday! So much for a quiet Sabbath! The three to take an early bath on 10th March 1974 were Steve Davey, Dave Provan and Bobby Saxton. The eight Argyle players left on the field, including Paul Mariner who broke his nose, were relieved to hear the final whistle. The inevitable 2-1 defeat could have been a lot worse, but for the fact that both Davey and Saxton were sent off late in the game.

Micky Horswill was sent off whilst playing for Plymouth Argyle in an abandoned game! He was sent packing by Exeter referee Ron Crabb for squaring up to, and then chasing, an opposing player in the 27th minute of the match against Bradford City at Home Park in February 1978. The match was later abandoned in the 61st minute due to the freezing conditions. Perhaps Horswill was merely trying to keep warm?

Preston North End created an unwanted club record when they had two players sent off in the match against Plymouth Argyle in September 1984. The miscreants were Tommy Booth and Jon Clark. The match was certainly not short of entertainment as Argyle won 6-4.

Argyle's goalkeeper and Player-Manager Peter Shilton was sent off for the first time in his long career, stretching back 26 years, in the Second Division fixture at Hull City in August 1992. Until then Shilton, who was appearing in the 1,336th League and Cup match of his career, had only been previously booked on two occasions. He was sent off in the 24th minute for a 'professional foul' bringing down Hull winger Graeme Atkinson. Nicky Marker took over between the posts but could do nothing, despite a gallant display, to prevent Hull scoring twice, Argyle losing 2-0.

SNOW

The Plymouth Argyle team made a fruitless journey to Coventry City in February 1947. The winter that year was to prove somewhat notorious being one of the worst for snow in living memory. On the day before the match was due to be played, a Coventry Corporation snowplough was called into Coventry City's Highfield Road ground in an attempt to clear five inches of snow from the pitch. This worked perfectly, but unfortunately the temperatures dropped so low overnight that by the Saturday morning the playing surface resembled a skating rink. The Argyle team which had stayed overnight at Birmingham, arrived at the ground to find the gates closed and notices chalked up reading 'Match Off'. They decided to head home and travelled by train back via London, making another overnight stop in the capital, arriving in Plymouth on Sunday afternoon. Club officials were not amused, for they reckoned the whole trip had cost between £80 and £100 for nothing.

Argyle's reserves didn't fare much better either, for on the same Saturday afternoon they were engaged in a Football Combination fixture at Bournemouth. They did at least play for 75 minutes though, trailing to a goal scored by Tunnicliffe, when the referee decided to abandon proceedings as the snow continued to fall, obliterating any pitch markings.

Two weeks later the Reserves defeated Swansea Town 3-1 back at Home Park. But the game only took place thanks to the efforts of the match referee Mr Edwards of Yeovil, who arrived at 7.30 a.m., the groundstaff, and a posse of schoolboy volunteers that the game went ahead at all. They spent the morning clearing the pitch of mini snowdrifts, particularly at the Devonport End of the ground.

SOUTHERN LEAGUE

Plymouth Argyle entered the Southern League in 1903/04, and remained members of the competition until joining the Football League. Argyle, however, retained a place in the Southern League by entering their reserves, staying until 1939.

The Southern League Championship was won by Argyle on five occasions in 1912/13, 1921/22, 1925/26, 1928/29 and 1933/34. In addition the runners-up place was attained in 1907/08, 1911/12, 1923/24, 1924/25, 1931/32 and 1937/38. It should be noted however that the league was split into two sections at one stage, with Argyle playing in the Western section in 1924, 1925 and 1932.

Plymouth Argyle became the first ever winners of the Southern League Cup, a competition which started in the 1932/33 season. Argyle had beaten Torquay United Reserves, Taunton Town, Llanelli and Bath City to reach the final. This was played over two legs, with Argyle drawing 0-0 at Folkestone Town, but defeating the Kent club in the return match at Home Park 6-3 to win the trophy. Argyle retained the cup the following season, beating Tunbridge Wells Rangers 4-1 on aggregate. The two clubs met each other again in the 1935/36 season final, and once more Argyle were triumphant winning 9-5 on aggregate.

Fellow members of the Southern League during Plymouth Argyle's first year in the competition in 1903 were: Brentford, Brighton & Hove Albion, Bristol Rovers, Fulham, Kettering Town, Luton Town, Millwall, New Brompton, Northampton Town, Portsmouth, Queens Park Rangers, Reading, Southampton, Swindon Town, Tottenham Hotspur, Wellingborough, and West Ham United.

Plymouth Argyle undertook their longest trip ever to fulfil a Southern League fixture on 12th October 1907 – to Yorkshire and Bradford! The ambitious Bradford Park Avenue club had taken the place of Fulham, who had been elected to the Football League. Park Avenue felt that the Southern League, despite the long journeys that they would have to undertake, was the best route for them to gain eventual Football League status themselves. Plymouth drew 0-0 at Bradford and won the return game 2-1 at Home Park the following February. Bradford Park Avenue's Football League ambitions were fulfilled the very next season.

A record attendance of twenty thousand for a match in the Southern League was set on Christmas day 1907 when Queens Park Rangers drew 0-0 at home to Plymouth Argyle.

In the 1938/39 season Plymouth Argyle Reserves netted 128 goals in their Southern League fixtures, but they still only managed to finish in fourth spot in the table, behind Colchester United, Guildford City and Gillingham.

SPOONER BROTHERS

The Spooner family played a major part in the formative years of Plymouth Argyle. Brothers Clarence, Guy, John and Stanley Spooner were already known in the city for their various business interests, and they became the leading protagonists behind introducing professional football to Plymouth. Stanley Spooner in particular was a real football enthusiast, so much so that when Argyle faced an early financial crisis in 1910 which threatened their very existence, he formed a new look board of directors, which included his brother Clarence, to take over the club.

The Spooner brothers are shown in the front row of this Plymouth Argyle photo of 1913/14. Back row (L to R) J. Kirkpatrick, J. Butler, W. Horne, S. Atterbury, W. Dixon. Third row (L to R) J. Bell, H. Raymond, F. Burch, H. Willcox, W. Baker, B. Bowler, T. Haynes, L. Crabb. Second row (L to R) B. S. Barrett, E. Harvey, A. Rogers, W. Sage, J. McCormick, A. Ham, A. Manico, E. Kelland, B. Jack. Front row (L to R) W. Olden, S. Quigley, J. D. Spooner, S. Spooner, A. Gard, B. Edmonds, A. J. Maunder.

Stanley also put up a magnificent trophy, known as the 'Spooner Cup', which was played for by Plymouth Argyle and Exeter City for a number of years. Exeter became the first holders of the cup when they won 1-0 at Home Park on 29th April 1914.

SUBSTITUTES

Full back John Hore became the first Plymouth Argyle player to take advantage of the newly introduced substitute rule in the 1965/66 season. He replaced the injured Frank Lord in a 1-1 draw at Charlton Athletic on 31st August 1965.

The first Argyle substitute to be used in a League fixture at Home Park was Duncan Neale. He took over from the injured Mike Bickle in the game against Crystal Palace on 11th April 1966. It was Bickle who scored Plymouth's goal in the 2-1 defeat.

Keith Etheridge became the first Argyle substitute to be called upon in an F.A. Cup tie, that being against Sheffield Wednesday in a third round tie at Hillsborough on 3rd January 1968.

In the Football League Cup first round match against Torquay United on 13th August 1969, Mike Bickle became the first Argyle substitute to be used in that particular competition. He replaced winger Aidan Maher, with the tie ending all square at 2-2.

SUNDAY SOCCER

The first occasion that Argyle played a competitive match on a Sunday occurred in March 1974 at Port Vale. It proved to be a disaster as no fewer than three Plymouth players were sent off by referee Kevin McNally of Blackpool. They were Steve Davey, Dave Provan and Bobby Saxton. This was the first time that three players from one side had ever been sent off in a Football League match.

The first Sunday Football League match to take place at Home Park was on 20th December 1987, when Brentford were the visitors for a Third Division fixture. The match had a noon kick off. The reasoning behind the switch from the more traditional Saturday afternoon fixture was the fact that the Home Park car park was in use for a Christmas Park and Ride shoppers service, thus there would have been no room for the usual matchday parking.

SUPPORTERS

Mr A. E. Cload was responsible for the Plymouth Argyle Supporters' Club being formed on 22nd January 1925. He was to become chairman and vice president, and in August 1946 accepted an invitation to join the Plymouth Argyle board of directors.

The Supporters' Club main aims at their formation was to raise much needed finance by organising a full programme of social gatherings and trips to away fixtures.

The Plymouth Argyle Supporters' Club became one of the founder members, in 1927, of the National Federation of Football Supporters' Clubs. The Federation then consisted of just six clubs, namely Brentford, Bournemouth and Boscombe Athletic, Brighton and Hove Albion, Charlton Athletic, Northampton Town and Plymouth Argyle.

Argyle's most famous supporter is probably Michael Foot. Elected leader of the Labour Party in 1980, he then said he had two ambitions, one to become Prime Minister, and two to see Argyle in the First Division. He remembers seeing his first match at Home Park in 1924, which was in the middle of the run when Argyle finished runners-up in the Third Division for six seasons. This prompted the inevitable talk among supporters that the

Ex-Labour Party Leader, Michael Foot, in the Argyle crowd.

club didn't really want promotion because of the added expense involved. Mr Foot remembers the disappointment of not being promoted until 1930. He followed Argyle throughout the 1930s never missing a home match first team or reserves. The first game that really stands out in his memory was the Christmas Day game at Tottenham who beat Argyle 2-1. His favourite player was goalscorer Sammy Black.

A London branch of the Supporters' Association was established on 30th June 1976. This flourishing branch boasted nearly 350 members by 1986, as well as issuing a monthly magazine called *Pasty News*. They have also since produced a *Third Division Travel Guide* and a *Great Mills League Guide* to assist supporters travelling to away matches, and a statistical booklet about Argyle. To celebrate the branch tenth anniversary, a celebration dinner was held at the Paddington Great Western Hotel.

Before the inaugural meeting held at The Ordnance Arms in St Johns Wood, London, Mr Sam Rendell, the Chairman of Plymouth Argyle Supporters' Association, said that they were pleased to learn that the name of Plymouth Argyle was being added to the growing number of clubs who have sections of their supporters' organisations in the London area.

There is also another equally active and enthusiastic group of Plymouth Argyle Supporters Trapped In Lancashire (PASTIL), formed in 1982 with a membership of about sixty.

TEAMS

Argyle have met a total of nine teams who have for one reason or another since lost their Football League status. The unfortunate clubs, some now just a mere memory, are Aberdare Athletic, Accrington Stanley, Aldershot, Barrow, Bradford Park Avenue, Colchester United, Merthyr Town, Newport County and Southport.

TELEVISION

Plymouth Argyle's Third Division fixture at Luton Town in January 1970 was featured on BBC Television's *Match Of The Day* programme. Only one member of the Argyle team cost the club a transfer fee, that being Aiden Maher who had been signed from Everton in October 1968 for £10,000. The Argyle team lined up as follows: Martin Clamp, Norman Piper, Colin Sullivan, David Lean, George Foster, John Hore, Steve Davey, Derek Rickard, Richard Reynolds, Mike Bickle, Aiden Maher. Plymouth put on a good show for the television viewers, winning 2-0 with goals from Bickle and Rickard.

Geoff Crudgington with Gazza lending a hand!

TESTIMONIALS

Popular Plymouth Argyle goalkeeper Geoff Crudgington, who made well over three hundred League appearances for the club, enjoyed a well earned testimonial match against Tottenham Hotspur at Home Park during the 1989/90 season. The Spurs paraded a galaxy of stars including Gary Lineker, Gary Mabbutt and the irrepressible Paul Gascoigne. An attendance of 8,652 witnessed a 3-0 victory for Spurs, with the goals being scored by Gascoigne, Mabbutt and an own goal from Argyle's Andy Morrison.

Another North London club to grace Home Park for a testimonial game was Spurs near neighbours, and great rivals, Arsenal. This was for long serving Plymouth Argyle secretary Graham Little in a pre-season meeting in 1991. Little had served Argyle as secretary for 26 years. To add to the occasion Arsenal paraded the Football League Championship Trophy before the game which they had won at the end of the 1990/91 season. For the record Argyle lost 2-0 before an attendance of 7,711 with Kevin Campbell and Alan Smith netting Arsenal goals.

TIPPERARY TUNE

The Plymouth Argyle squad recorded a record in 1975 to the tune of 'It's a long way to Tipperary'. The words were written by Argyle supporter Peter Twining of St Austell, whilst the musical backing was provided by the Mount Charles Silver Band. The opening verse went:

It's a long way to Plymouth Argyle
It's a long way to go
It's a long way down to Home Park
To watch Argyle steal the show.

TORQUAY UNITED

The Argyle have played at Torquay United's Plainmoor ground on numerous occasions, but they have also met Exeter City there in a competitive match. Plymouth and Exeter had been drawn against each other in the first round of the Football League Cup in the 1968/69 season, and it was to prove a titanic struggle before a winning team emerged.

The first meeting took place at Home Park in front of 8,862 spectators and ended in a goalless stalemate. The replay, a week later at Exeter City's St James's Park, still failed to resolve the issue, when once again neither side found the back of the net, in a game watched by 13,432. A second replay on the neutral ground of Torquay United's Plainmoor finally produced a winner, but not before the game again went into extra-time. Exeter's midfielder John Kirkham broke the deadlock in front of a crowd of 10,884 to earn the Grecians a second round meeting with First Division Sheffield Wednesday.

A number of players have been transferred between Plymouth Argyle and Torquay United. In fact no fewer than 27 players have made the short move from Home Park to Plainmoor since 1920 on a permanent transfer between the respective clubs. In addition there have been players who joined Torquay for a loan spell from Argyle. The players who have been transferred up until the commencement of the 1992/93 season include: Peter Anderson (1962), Pat Corcoran (1926), Terry Dann (1962), Peter Darke (1977), Harold Dobbie (1953), Alec Edmunds (1928), Mike Green (1977), Dave Hancock (1959), Billy Kellock (1920), Jimmy Kirkpatrick (1924), Tony Levy (1979), John Matthews (1989), Glyn Nicholas (1966), Fred Preskett (1937), Bob Preston (1928), Harry Raymond (1924), John Sims (1983), Jack Smith (1954) Bob Smith (1927), Ellis Stuttard (1947), Tommy Tynan (1990), John Uzzell (1989), Bruce Wallace (1925), Dave Walter (1992),

Peter Whiston (1990), John Williams (1962) and Reg Wyatt (1964).

Players being transferred from Torquay United to Plymouth Argyle include: Eric Burgess (1968), Ernie Edds (1953), Morton Morgan (1937), Donal Murphy (1980), Bob Preston (1923) and Alan Welsh (1972).

Harry Raymond, who moved from Plymouth to Torquay United in 1924, joined the Plainmoor club as Player-Manager. Torquay were at that time still playing their first team football in the Southern League. Raymond, an England amateur international, had originally signed for Argyle in 1908 from local club Woodland Villa.

One of the more unusual meetings between Torquay United and Plymouth Argyle took place at Plainmoor in 1925. The receipts resulting from the friendly fixture went towards a fund set up by the Torquay club to help pay for repairs to the grandstand roof which had been severely damaged in storms.

UNBEATEN

A remarkable unbeaten home run of matches began with an undistinguished goalless draw with Southampton at Home Park on 2nd April 1921. For it was to be another fifty league and cup matches before Plymouth Argyle were defeated in front of their own supporters. The team that ended the record were Portsmouth, who won 2-1, this being the opening home league fixture of the season on 25th August 1923. Argyle had gone 47 league and three cup fixtures without defeat.

Argyle went unbeaten for a club record 22 matches between 20th April 1929 and 25th December 1929. After beating Luton Town 2-0 at Home Park, the next team to dent Plymouth's remarkable run was Coventry City, who won 1-0 at their Highfield Road ground.

UNBREAKABLE

Before Plymouth Argyle ordered 3,437 seats for their Lyndhurst Stand in 1992, the club's Chief Executive Liz Baker wanted to ensure the manufacturers' claims that the said seats were unbreakable were true. Liz, along with a little help, tested five different companies' seats. They jumped up and down on them, two people at a time. They tried to bend them out of shape by hand. Liz explained that the tests were designed to represent normal wear and tear, and was concerned that any seats to be installed should meet certain criteria. The seats, at a cost of £60,000, were installed in time for the commencement of the 1992/93 season.

UNITED STATES

A party of two Plymouth Argyle directors, manager Jimmy Rae, and trainer George Taylor, and fifteen players, undertook a ten match tour in twenty five days of the United States at the end of the 1953/54 season. It proved to be, in terms of results, and despite the enormous amount of

The Argyle contingent who left Plymouth in 1954 to play a series of matches in the United States of America.

travelling, an extremely successful tour with only two defeats. In one match against a Colorado All Stars XI, Sam McCrory netted six goals as Argyle romped to an easy victory! Their complete tour record, showing the venue of each game, was as follows: Borussia Dortmund (Chicago) Lost 0-4; St Louis Simkins (St Louis) Won 8-4; Colorado All Stars (Denver) Won 16-2; Borussia Dortmund (Los Angeles) Lost 1-3; Los Angeles Scots (Los Angeles) Won 2-0; San Francisco All Stars (San Francisco) Won 2-0; Chicago All Stars (Chicago) Won 8-1; Chicago Polish Falcons (Detroit) Won 6-1; Philadelphia All Stars (Philadelphia) Won 3-2; American All Stars (New York) Won 1-0.

Borussia Dortmund were the West German League Champions and were in the United States at the same time as Argyle. An attendance of twelve thousand watched the first encounter between the respective teams, with an even better fifteen thousand spectators being present for the return match in a Los Angeles baseball stadium.

VICE-PRESIDENTS

A Plymouth Argyle Vice-Presidents' Club was formed in 1969, with the membership initially limited to one hundred persons. This was increased to 150 following the enlargement of the Vice-Presidents' premises at Home Park. As well as providing an ideal meeting place for matches and indeed during the week, the Vice-Presidents also proved to be a valuable source of income for Argyle, who received donations in the region of £35,000 during the first ten years of the Vice-Presidents' Club's existence.

WESTERN LEAGUE

Plymouth Argyle have had a long association with the Western League, although they have left, only to later rejoin the competition on four occasions. Argyle's first team became members of the Western League Division One for the 1903/04 season, playing such teams as Tottenham Hotspur, Southampton, Queens Park Rangers and West Ham United! The league then contained many illustrious clubs, who played both in the Southern and Western Leagues. Apart from those mentioned, other teams that Argyle met in their first season of Western League football were Brentford, Bristol Rovers, Portsmouth and Reading. Argyle ended their first spell in the Western League in 1909.

Argyle's reserve team played in the Western League between 1925 and 1932. They actually won the Western League First Division Championship in their final season, 1931/32, but then withdrew from the competition and so did not defend their title. They had won the title by two points from runners-up Yeovil and Petters United.

The Argyle 'A' team enjoyed a couple of seasons as members of the Western League between 1967 and 1969. More recently the reserves, after dropping out of the Football Combination, entered the league again in 1982.

Plymouth have registered over a hundred goals in a season in Western League football on two occasions – 105 in 1987/88 and 100 in 1990/91. On the other hand, Argyle have never conceded a hundred goals or more.

Including and up to the end of the 1991/92 season, Plymouth Argyle's complete record in Western League football stood at: Played 688, Won 318, Drew 149, Lost 221, For 1,378, Against 936.

WHY ARGYLE?

One of the most often asked questions among football supporters is how Plymouth acquired the name 'Argyle'. In fact Plymouth almost did not lay claim to being the first senior club to adopt the name Argyle. Glasgow Rangers Football Club, who were formed in 1872, actually played one match as Glasgow Argyle. Then one of the founder members of the club spotted the name Rangers in a rugby union manual, liked the sound of it, and changed the name from Glasgow Argyle to Glasgow Rangers. Therefore Argyle, the Plymouth variety, today has become the unique name of the Devon club in both the Football League and Scottish League. There have been several explanations over the years, but the most probable explanation is as described in a letter from Howard Grose, the first captain of Argyle in the 1886/87 season, written from Southsea on 25th March 1934, which said:

My dear Pascho
I was very pleased indeed to hear from you ...
... and now about "Plymouth Argyle". Its story is woven with mine somewhat so you must excuse me writing in the first person. I left

Dunheved College, Launceston in 1885 where with my friend and colleague, Mr W. Pethybridge I took keen interest in football and cricket. Mr Pethybridge left school before me and took up the study of law with a firm of solicitors in Plymouth. I joined him there early in 1886 to learn architecture and engineering. We wished to take an active part in our favourite sports in Plymouth and to that end often discussed what club we could join but outside the Plymouth Town Football Club there was none that appealed to us. I think it was Mr Pethybridge who first suggested that it might be possible to form a new club by recruiting The Old Boys from the neighbouring public schools and colleges: we knew several promising young men of this class engaged in study or business in the town and determined to approach them on the subject. The majority showed themselves keenly interested in the proposal and the first conference took place in our rooms which Mr Pethybridge and I jointly occupied – when it was arranged to call a meeting for the purpose of forming a club. The meeting took place at the Borough Arms and it was decided to form a club such as we had in mind. The question of what name the club should be known by then arose and that of "Pickwick" was mentioned and found favour with several present: others however objected as the name did not adapt itself to local application. I recollect holding forth on what our club should aim at achieving in the football world viz: to emulate the style of play adopted by the Argyll and Sutherland Highlanders who I believe in the previous year won The Army Cup (this no doubt can be verified). I then explained that anyone who had watched them play would have been struck with the excellent team work shown, the fast low passing from backs to forwards, wings to centre followed by short swift shooting at the opponents' goal etc. and we should endeavour to play on the same lines. Then someone said "why not a 'Plymouth Argyll'? That's a name that could be applied locally." The suggestion was well received and when put to the vote was adopted almost unanimously. Subsequently the meeting elected me as the first Captain of the new club for the season 1886/7.

We had no club ground at first and were obliged to play matches on our opponents' grounds. The team exercised on the then Freedom Fields (now Freedom Park) and so eager were members to get into condition that I remember several games taking place there by moonlight. Later in the season permission was obtained to play on a ground at Mount Gould where several matches took place. From newspaper cuttings still in my possession it appears that the first match played was against 'Caxton' on Oct. 16th 1886 which was lost by 4 goals to 2 – on Oct. 30 1886 we played the Plymouth College which Argyle won by 2-1. The college side was captained by Mr Babb who later in the season joined our club on leaving the college. During this season 17 matches were played, 7 were won, 8 lost and 2 drawn. This record for the first season was considered highly satisfactory as the team had previously no means of playing together and it took some time for individual members to find their proper place of play on the field and get licked into shape ...

...The membership of the club increased rapidly and in January 1887 a second eleven was organised and matches arranged. The second team did exceptionally well and won most of the games played.

For the season 1889/90, Mr Babb being absent, the records show that F. H. Grose was elected captain with Mr W. C. Hawke sub-captain, C. W. Phillips Hon. Treasurer and H. M. Gibson Hon. Secretary. The teams had a successful season and won the majority of the matches played. Out of 15 matches played, 11 were won, 73 goals scored for the club and 15 against – a record that many clubs might envy today.

I left the district in 1890 and regret that I cannot assist you in the subsequent history of the Argyle. I recollect however in the latter part of this season we left the Mount Gould site and acquired a football ground at Marsh Mills where I played in several matches.

...

with kindest regards and best wishes
Yours sincerely
(signed) F. Howard Grose

It is also recorded that the Argyle Athletic Club was originally formed in 1888 following a meeting in a house situated in Argyll Terrace, Mutley, Plymouth. The football section of the club gradually became more and more popular until it became the predominant sporting activity.

What is clear, however, is that the Argyle Athletic Club's football section really flourished, along with a newly-formed cricket section of the club. They rented premises under a shop in the Mutley area which were used as their headquarters, with both social gatherings and committee meetings being held there.

Although it is not entirely clear just how the name 'Argyle' did get chosen, there is little doubt that it has proved to be a good choice. Because it is unique, football fans throughout the country immediately think of Plymouth when the word 'Argyle' is mentioned. The Argyle Athletic Club moved their football ground to Home Park in 1901, and the name of Plymouth Argyle was adopted on introducing professionalism two years later.

It was at a meeting held on 8th January 1903 at Chubb's Hotel, Plymouth that a decision was taken by the Argyle Athletic Club to form a separate company to run the football section of their activities. The name of the company would be Plymouth Argyle Association Football Club Limited.

Minutes of meetings from those formative times, state that the new company had a capital of £3,000 divided into £1 shares. Only two thousand were issued at first with Mr Clarence Spooner, Chairman of the Argyle Athletic Club, adding that it was his intention to become one of the major shareholders.

The first board of directors was duly elected as follows: Lieutenant F. Windrum (Chairman), Messrs A. V. Adlard, A. Corderoy, R. F. Davis, G. Shillabear, C. N. Spooner and J. D. Spooner

Within days Mr Shillabear resigned from the newly formed board and was replaced by Mr A. C. Godfrey.

'X-RATED'

Plymouth Argyle, like most clubs, have been on the wrong end of humiliating F.A. Cup defeats, although they have only twice ever lost to a non-league team. On the first occasion Argyle lost 3-1 in the North East at South Shields in the first round in January 1927. More recently Plymouth had to travel to Southern League Worcester City in November 1978 for a first round tie. The partisan attendance of 8,253 roared their team on to a famous 2-0 win over the Argyle. Club secretary Graham Little described the coach journey back to Devon as "the quietest I have ever known."

Only one other non-league club has come close to an F.A. Cup upset against Argyle. Ironically it was twelve months earlier than the Worcester game, for Plymouth were once again drawn away in the first round, this time to another Southern League side of previous F.A. Cup renown, Bath City. Plymouth were held to a goalless draw at Twerton Park, but made sure of a place in the next round by winning the replay back at Home Park thanks to a couple of goals from Brian Taylor.

Against Hendon in the first round of the Cup in 1972/73 it was 0-0 with three minutes to go and a replay on the Londoners' ground looked almost certain, but up popped Neil Hague to net what proved to be the winning goal.

The great Escape! 2-1 down with just a few minutes to go at Dartford, again in the first round, but this time in 1974/75. Argyle made a match-saving, and indeed winning, substitution however, by sending on winger Alan Rogers who promptly supplied two pin point crosses which led to a face-saving comeback and a 3-2 win for Plymouth.

YEOVIL TOWN

Plymouth Argyle first met Yeovil Town (then known as Yeovil and Petters United) in a competitive match in 1922/23. The Argyle reserve team and the Yeovil club were then playing in the Southern League, which at that time was split into an English and Welsh section. The two clubs have of course met each other on numerous occasions since then.

Argyle's first team crossed paths with Yeovil and Petters United for the

first time in November 1928, when a crowd of over ten thousand packed into the Huish ground for an F.A. Cup tie. Plymouth ran out fairly easy winners by 4-1, with two goals from Ray Bowden, and one each netted by Jack Leslie and Alf Matthews.

ZERO

Goal famines strike clubs from time to time, and the worst run that Plymouth Argyle have experienced in Football League fixtures has been five games without a goal. This has occurred on three occasions, in seasons 1938/39, 1947/48 and 1949/50. The worst start to a season in the league as far as Argyle and goals are concerned, came in the opening four matches of the 1981/82 season. Not a goal was scored, whilst four were conceded.

Argyle's record number of Football League games without conceding a goal stands at six. This happened in season 1924/25, Argyle winning five of them and drawing the other, scoring twelve goals themselves without reply.

Exeter City: A File of Fascinating Football Facts
Mike Blackstone   **112 pages**   **£4.95**

Exeter City may well be synonymous with the colours Red and White, but they have changed their colours more times than a chameleon! Exeter City have played in Green and White, Chocolate and Yellow, Tangerine and Black, all Red, all White and even Sky Blue! Needless to say, Exeter City have had a colourful past in more ways than one and this 'file of fascinating football facts' records numerous odd and nearly forgotten stories.

Memories will be revived as Mike Blackstone delves into his extensive collection of football memorabilia. He recalls when 'Tarzan' played in goal for the City, retells the saga of the club's very own 'dead parrot sketch' and recollects the International fixture between Brazil and Exeter City.

If you have enjoyed Mike Blackstone's Argyle book, then this 'sister' book is a must for your bookshelf.

Torquay United – the first 70 years
Laura Joint   **96 pages**   **£4.95**

Torquay United may be one of the smallest clubs in the Football League, but it has a proud history which spans three score years and ten. Laura Joint, Torquay United correspondent on the Western Morning News, has captured and chronicled the ups and downs, the joys and despairs of the Gulls' colourful past in this entertainingly informative book.

Football enthusiasts can now relive some of the club's most memorable matches and incidents, and read about the characters who have helped to shape its history. Here is a permanent reminder of both the good times and bad for fans and followers who have enjoyed and endured the fluctuating fortunes of Torquay United.

Both the above books are available from Obelisk Publications, 2 Church Hill, Pinhoe, Exeter, EX4 9ER, priced £4.95, post & packing free. SPECIAL OFFER: Buy one book, get the other one half price! For both books, send cheque/P.O. for just £7.50 (payable to Obelisk Publications) with your name and address.